The Great Depression

Titles in the World History Series

The Age of Feudalism
The American Frontier
Ancient Greece
The Ancient Near East
Architecture
Aztec Civilization
Caesar's Conquest of Gaul
The Crusades
The Cuban Revolution
The Early Middle Ages
Egypt of the Pharaohs
Elizabethan England
The End of the Cold War
The French and Indian War
The French Revolution
The Glorious Revolution
The Great Depression
Greek and Roman Theater
Hitler's Reich
The Hundred Years' War
The Inquisition
The Italian Renaissance
The Late Middle Ages
The Lewis and Clark Expedition
Modern Japan
The Punic Wars
The Reformation
The Relocation of the North American Indian
The Roman Empire
The Roman Republic
The Russian Revolution
Traditional Africa
Traditional Japan
The Travels of Marco Polo
The Wars of the Roses
Women's Suffrage

Dedicated to John and Mary Farrell, who survived the Great Depression. In the late 1920s, they came to the United States from the Republic of Ireland. They lived through the rough times examined in this book. And they taught their daughter that, in spite of its problems, America is still the land of opportunity.

WORLD HISTORY SERIES ∎∎∎

The Great Depression

by
Jacqueline Farrell

Lucent Books, P.O. Box 289011, San Diego, CA 92198-9011

Library of Congress Cataloging-in-Publication Data

Farrell, Jacqueline 1951–
   The great depression / by Jacqueline Farrell
      p. cm.—(World history series)
   Includes bibliographical references and index.
   ISBN 1-56006-276-2 (lib. ed : alk. paper)
   1. New Deal, 1933-1939—Juvenile literature. 2. Depres-
sions—1929—United States—Juvenile literature. 3. United
States—History—1933-1945—Juvenile literature.
[1. Depressions—1929. 2. United States—History—1933-1945.]
I.Title. II. Series.
E806.F264   1996
973.917—dc20   95-11709
                                        CIP
                                       AC

Contents

Foreword   8

Important Dates in the History of
the Great Depression   10

INTRODUCTION
We Were Poor   12

CHAPTER 1
The Roots of the Depression   15

CHAPTER 2
Hoover and Roosevelt   23

CHAPTER 3
The First Hundred Days   34

CHAPTER 4
A New Deal on the Farm and in the City   46

CHAPTER 5
The Debate Between Recovery and Reform   60

CHAPTER 6
The Worldwide Depression   68

CHAPTER 7
The Legacy of the Depression   80

Notes   85
For Further Reading   87
Works Consulted   88
Index   91
Picture Credits   96
About the Author   96

Foreword

Each year on the first day of school, nearly every history teacher faces the task of explaining why his or her students should study history. One logical answer to this question is that exploring what happened in our past explains how the things we often take for granted—our customs, ideas, and institutions—came to be. As statesman and historian Winston Churchill put it, "Every nation or group of nations has its own tale to tell. Knowledge of the trials and struggles is necessary to all who would comprehend the problems, perils, challenges, and opportunities which confront us today." Thus, a study of history puts modern ideas and institutions in perspective. For example, though the founders of the United States were talented and creative thinkers, they clearly did not invent the concept of democracy. Instead, they adapted some democratic ideas that had originated in ancient Greece and with which the Romans, the British, and others had experimented. An exploration of these cultures, then, reveals their very real connection to us through institutions that continue to shape our daily lives.

Another reason often given for studying history is the idea that lessons exist in the past from which contemporary societies can benefit and learn. This idea, although controversial, has always been an intriguing one for historians. Those that agree that society can benefit from the past often quote philosopher George Santayana's famous statement, "Those who cannot remember the past are condemned to repeat it." Historians who ascribe to Santayana's philosophy believe that, for example, studying the events that led up to the major world wars or other significant historical events would allow society to chart a different and more favorable course in the future.

Just as difficult as convincing students to realize the importance of studying history is the search for useful and interesting supplementary materials that present historical events in a context that can be easily understood. The volumes in Lucent Books' World History Series attempt to present a broad, balanced, and penetrating view of the march of history. Ancient Egypt's important wars and rulers, for example, are presented against the rich and colorful backdrop of Egyptian religious, social, and cultural developments. The series engages the reader by enhancing historical events with these cultural contexts. For example, in *Ancient Greece*, the text covers the role of women in that society. Slavery is discussed in *The Roman Empire*, as well as how slaves earned their freedom. The numerous and varied aspects of everyday life in these and other societies are explored in each volume of the series. Additionally, the series covers the major political, cultural, and philosophical ideas as the torch of civilization is passed from ancient Mesopotamia and Egypt, through Greece, Rome, Medieval Europe, and other world cultures, to the modern day.

The material in the series is formatted in a thorough, precise, and organized manner. Each volume offers the reader a comprehensive and clearly written overview of an important historical event or period. The topic under discussion is placed in a broad historical context. For example, *The Italian Renaissance* begins with a discussion of the High Middle Ages and the loss of central control that allowed certain Italian cities to develop artistically. The book ends by looking forward to the Reformation and interpreting the societal changes that grew out of the Renaissance. Thus, students are not only involved in an historical era, but also enveloped by the events leading up to that era and the events following it.

One important and unique feature in the World History Series is the primary and secondary source quotations that richly supplement each volume. These quotes are useful in a number of ways. First, they allow students access to sources they would not normally be exposed to because of the difficulty and obscurity of the original source. The quotations range from interesting anecdotes to far-sighted cultural perspectives and are drawn from historical witnesses both past and present. Second, the quotes demonstrate how and where historians themselves derive their information on the past as they strive to reach a consensus on historical events. Lastly, all of the quotes are footnoted, familiarizing students with the citation process and allowing them to verify quotes and/or look up the original source if the quote piques their interest.

Finally, the books in the World History Series provide a detailed launching point for further research. Each book contains a bibliography specifically geared toward student research. A second annotated bibliography introduces students to all the sources the author consulted when compiling the book. A chronology of important dates gives students an overview, at a glance, of the topic covered. Where applicable, a glossary of terms is included.

In short, the series is designed not only to acquaint readers with the basics of history, but also to make them aware that their lives are a part of an ongoing human saga. Perhaps they will then come to the same realization as famed historian Arnold Toynbee. In his monumental work, *A Study of History*, he wrote about becoming aware of history flowing through him in a mighty current, and of his own life "welling like a wave in the flow of this vast tide."

Important Dates in the History of the Great Depression

1919	1927	1928	1929	1930	193

1919
The Treaty of Versailles ends World War I; its terms demand full reparations and payment of war debts from the defeated countries.

1927
Some American banks fail because of bad investments and low prices for agricultural produce.

1928
Herbert Hoover, an advocate of rugged individualism, is elected president of the United States.

1929
The American stock market fails in October, and millions of investors are plunged into bankruptcy.

1930
The Hawley-Smoot Tariff Act raises import duties on a variety of industrial products and raw materials.

1931
Hostilities begin between Japan and China; the resulting increase in defense spending and war preparations effectively insulates Japan from the economic depression felt in other industrial nations; Hoover creates the Reconstruction Finance Corporation to lend money to banks and businesses to prevent them from failing.

1932
Franklin Delano Roosevelt is elected president of the United States.

1933
Adolf Hitler becomes chancellor of Germany and puts into effect his four-year plan of economic recovery; Roosevelt declares a federal bank holiday to determine which are solvent enough to reopen; FDR broadcasts first fireside chat with America; the One Hundred Days congressional session approves fifteen major acts, thus initiating the New Deal; the World Economic Conference in London fails to agree on policies of international cooperation to combat the worldwide depression.

1934

The Securities and Exchange Act regulates Wall Street trading; the Democratic majorities in Congress and state governments in midterm elections are seen as a mandate for extending New Deal policies.

1935

The National Labor Relations Act gives workers the right to organize; the Social Security Act provides for old-age pensions and unemployment insurance; Italy invades Ethiopia; the continuing military buildup ends Italy's economic depression.

1936

Germany's second four-year plan focuses on defense spending and the buildup of arms.

1937

Franklin Delano Roosevelt begins second term as president of the United States; the recession of 1937–1938 begins, and unemployment rises to 20 percent of American workers; Congress defeats the Supreme Court Reform Bill, emphasizing that the Constitution must remain the guiding principle of the government.

1939

Germany invades Czechoslovakia, and the resulting defense spending and arms buildup by Great Britain, France, and the United States ends the Great Depression of the 1930s.

We Were Poor

In the winter of 1932 the most popular song on the radio was "Brother Can You Spare a Dime?" It told the story of a man who had lost his job and suddenly found himself begging for money on the street.

An unemployed man peddles apples for a nickel during the Great Depression in an effort to earn enough money for life's necessities.

He had desperately tried to find work, but to no avail. The lyrics reflected his anger at being unable to make a contribution to his country:

> Once I built a railroad, made it run
> Made it race against time.
> Once I built a railroad, now it's done.
> Brother can you spare a dime?[1]

The song was popular because it reflected the plight of millions of people. America was three years into the Great Depression. Economic crises were nothing new in the United States. In the 1830s, 1870s, and 1890s, there had been years when prices of goods fell, unemployment rose, wages were cut, and production was down. These events were categorized with natural disasters, like droughts or blizzards, and no one had been able to explain their causes. Both government and industry believed that they would eventually run their course and recovery would come. And economic recovery had always come. However, the depression of the 1930s was more severe than any of the others, and this time it lasted for ten years.

After the prosperity of the 1920s, most Americans were in shock when factories, stores, and mines closed down. People who had never been out of work found themselves living in poverty, and they could not quite believe that this was happening to them. The thirteen-year-old son of a mill worker spoke for many when he told an interviewer from the Federal Writers' Project how he felt when his father lost his job:

> We were really up against it. For a whole week one time we didn't have anything to eat but potatoes. Another time my brother went around to grocery stores and got them to give him meat for his dog—only he didn't have a dog. We ate that dog meat with the potatoes. I went to school hungry and came home to a house where there wasn't any fire. The lights were cut off. . . . I remember lying in bed one night and thinking. All at once I realized something. We were poor. Lord! It was weeks before I could get over that. I was ashamed to look at anybody and to talk to them.[2]

Almost twelve million Americans were unemployed in 1932. Most of them had been out of work for so long that their savings had run out. Eventually they lost

Depression-era photographer Dorothea Lange captured the desperation of a poor migrant family in this memorable 1936 picture.

their homes when they could not pay their rent or mortgages. Many lived in communities of cardboard shacks called Hoovervilles. Breadlines providing bread

Evicted from their homes and apartments, some unemployed people fashioned shelters from cardboard and lumber scraps. Called Hoovervilles, entire communities of these shacks sprung up on the edges of cities.

and soup for the poor were established in every town, and hospitals distributed their leftover food. Thousands of young men and boys became hoboes, traveling back and forth across the country looking for temporary jobs. A third of a million children were out of school because their communities could not afford to keep the schools open.

Three years of hunger and poverty had left Americans with little hope but many questions. What had caused the economic crisis? Should the government step in and provide for its citizens when those citizens could do nothing for themselves? Attempts to answer these questions changed the relationship between the U.S. government and the American people.

1 The Roots of the Depression

Even though the Allied powers of Great Britain, France, and the Soviet Union had been the European military victors in World War I, their economies were devastated by it. Recovering from the war economically proved to be a more difficult task than winning the war militarily. The Allied nations were heavily in debt, and their resources had been depleted because of the high cost of paying for the war. In addition, Europe's major cities and industries had been destroyed and required rebuilding. And for the duration of the war European industries had focused on producing armaments and military supplies. Now these factories needed to be reconverted for civilian industry. In Europe this was more difficult because of international trade competition.

During the war Asia and South America had become much more industrialized to provide consumer products to Europe, which could not maintain its industries during the war. When the war ended, Asia and South America continued to produce and export steel, silk, petroleum, and other consumer items to Europe. This resulted in less demand for European and American goods and continued to delay European economic recovery.

An elderly French couple visits their former home in a region devastated by the Germans during World War I. European cities destroyed during the war required costly rebuilding.

Germany was just as hard hit as the other European nations but faced additional burdens. The Treaty of Versailles, which ended the war, stipulated that the entire cost of the war, $186 billion, must be paid by Germany, Austria-Hungary, Turkey, and Bulgaria. The debt had to be paid in foreign securities—that is, non-German stocks, bonds, and currencies—and in consumer products. Since Germany could not afford to purchase these monies, it attempted to pay the other countries with German products. However, the other nations soon realized that if they accepted German products in payment, they would have to sell the products to their own citizens. This availability of inexpensive German products would mean that the home industries of the other European nations would not sell as many goods and would have to lay off workers.

Finding an acceptable means of allowing Germany to pay its debts seemed an insurmountable problem. Finally, an international committee led by American banker Charles G. Dawes developed a solution. Agreed upon in April 1924, the Dawes Plan provided for a schedule of Germany's reparation, or compensation, payments. In addition, the United States agreed to loan money to Germany in order to stabilize its economy. Even with the plan, however, Germany's economy was years away from recovery.

Agriculture also suffered in the transition from a wartime to civilian economy. Improved farm machinery and developments of fertilizers, pesticides, and hardier varieties of plants greatly increased the amount of food grown. During the war the United States, Canada, Australia, and South American countries had increased

The Dawes Plan, editorialized in this cartoon, allowed Germany to pay its huge World War I debt with a schedule of payments.

production in order to feed not only their own people, but the Europeans as well. After the war these nations did not cut back on their farm productivity even though European farmers resumed production. The supply of food exceeded market demand. The prices of food fell, and farming became less profitable. When farmers made less money, they had less money to invest or to spend on consumer goods, and the rest of the economy suffered as well.

American agriculture was especially hurt in this transition. During World War I American farmers had taken out mortgages to buy more land and equipment so they could produce more food and reap bigger profits. When food prices fell, American farmers could not repay these mortgages. Those unpaid loans would reverberate in the banking industry and contribute to the depression.

Benefits to the United States

In other ways, however, the United States greatly benefited from the situation after World War I. Because American industry had escaped destruction, the nation had a head start on converting its economy from one focused on war to one focused on consumer production. Factories previously devoted to producing armaments now produced automobiles, radios, and household appliances. Industry expanded to produce luxuries, not just necessities. To create a market for these goods, U.S. businesses developed and promoted buying on credit. Before credit became available, a buyer would have to save to pay the full amount for a car, radio, or washing machine. With credit, a person could make a small deposit, take the product home, and pay for it in monthly installments. Although credit was good for business, it had adverse effects on the banking and investment industries because it dis-

couraged people from saving. Bankers then had less money to invest worldwide.

Throughout the 1920s American businesses prospered because of a frenzy of spending on the new consumer goods. Americans became optimistic that this prosperity would continue indefinitely. In his final message to Congress in 1929, President Calvin Coolidge expressed his faith in American business:

> The great wealth created by our enterprise and industry, and saved by our economy, has had the widest distribution among our own people, and has gone out in a steady stream to serve the charity and business of the world. The requirements of existence have passed beyond the standard of necessity into the region of luxury. . . . The country can regard the present with satisfaction and anticipate the future with optimism.[3]

But the emphasis on the production of luxuries, not necessities, meant that continued prosperity was only as secure as the jobs of the consumers. If one factory laid off workers, those workers were unable to buy the goods produced by other workers, who then lost their jobs. This tenuous situation could be easily endangered by a downturn in the economy.

International political trends affected the American economy, as well. The economy had become more international after World War I, as nations' trade and money became more intermingled. Nations of the world did not recognize this, however. Many nations, including the United States, remained extremely nationalistic, concerned more about their own nation's recovery. As Robert S. McElvaine noted in *The Great Depression:*

> By the late twenties, each country was seeking to advance its own interests, even if in the process it worsened the position of the others. In a delicate, interdependent world economy, these "beggar-thy-neighbor" tactics were suicidal. Nowhere should this have been more clear than in the United States. This country was trying nothing less in the 1920s than to be the world's banker, food producer, and manufacturer, but to buy as little as possible from the world in return.[4]

Because the United States had emerged from the war unscathed, it became the world's leading creditor nation because it was prosperous enough to lend money to other countries. Historians fault the United States for not having assumed leadership and taken more responsibility in moderating the world economy and promoting free trade among nations. Instead of stimulating other nations' economies, the United States, like other nations, promoted only its own recovery. The United States refused to join the League of Nations and retreated into a second period of isolationism. Even when America agreed to lend money to Europe through the Dawes Plan, its industrial leaders were more interested in obtaining profits for bankers than in stabilizing the world economy. After American investors saw how profitable international loans could be, they began to offer money to other nations. But investors refused to see

During the 1920s, the United States increased production of luxury items like automobiles, radios, and household appliances. To make these items more accessible to the masses, U.S. businesses began promoting buying on credit.

that in doing this they made European economic recovery more and more dependent on the continued prosperity of the United States.

The United States Backs Away from Leadership

Economist Charles P. Kindleberger asserted that a major cause of the depression was America's refusal to assume leadership in the financial markets of the world:

> The world economic system was unstable unless some country stabilized it, as Britain had done in the nineteenth century and up to 1913. In 1929, the English couldn't and the United States wouldn't. When every country turned to protect its national private interest, the world public interest went down the drain, and with it the private interests of all.[5]

Because of the amount of influence the American economy had in the world, the U.S. stock market was equally important to the world economy. When investors buy stock, they purchase shares in the ownership of that company. Long-term investors buy the stock because they hope that the company's business will be good and that it will make a lot of profits over the years. They will then be entitled to a share of those profits. Short-term investors hope that the cost of the share of stock will go up quickly so that they can sell the stock for more money and make a profit from reselling the stock. In the late 1920s many short-term investors were borrowing money to purchase stocks on

The New York Stock Exchange on Wall Street (pictured during the 1929 crash) is the nation's largest and most influential stock exchange.

credit, a practice known as buying on margin. If the stock went up, they could repay the money and still have some profit. But if the price went down, they did not make enough profit to repay the loan. The bank or broker who had made the loan lost money. In turn, the bank or broker would demand immediate payment from other lenders who could pay. This led to a frenzy of selling, with people taking whatever they could get for their stocks. As a result, overall prices of stocks went down. And the more prices fell, the more people wanted to sell their stocks.

Prices did not go down as long as people continued to purchase goods and services and have confidence in the nation's economic health. However, by 1929 speculating in the stock market had become more profitable than actually investing in a company's product and waiting to share in its future profits. This increased the demand for stock. With so many interested buyers available, prices of stocks rose. These inflated stock prices were based on buyer demand, not on the actual productivity and profits of the company. To make money on such stocks, the investor would have to quickly sell the stock to another investor. Unscrupulous stockbrokers were increasingly willing to prey on the greed and get-rich hopes of thousands of small investors and continued to sell stocks on margin, even though they knew the prices were inflated.

In response to the speculative buying and selling of stocks on margin, some bankers and politicians urged the Federal Reserve Board, the government agency that advises the nation's banks, to increase the interest rates so that borrowing for investments would become less profitable. The Federal Reserve Board responded by suggesting that banks reduce the amount of money available for loans, but it could not require the banks to act because the American free enterprise system at that time rejected the practice of government regulation of business. Most of the banks were privately owned and did not have to prove to any government agency that they were wisely investing their depositors' money. Therefore, most banks ignored the Federal Reserve and continued to lend money to brokers who wanted to sell stocks on margin.

By expressing their confidence in continued American prosperity, government financial experts and leaders such as Presi-

---

American Isolationism

President Calvin Coolidge was a strong supporter of business, and his term became known as the era of Coolidge prosperity. During this time the average American ignored what was going on in the rest of the world. In his book Shattered Decade, *historian Irving Weinstein notes:*

"With conditions so good at home, Americans shut their eyes to the rest of the world, no matter what momentous events occurred. Lenin's death in 1924 and the power struggle that followed it in Russia passed almost unnoticed by Americans. The growing political unrest in Germany meant nothing to them. No attention was paid to the withdrawal of French troops from the Ruhr Valley and its return to German control. Nor did many Americans bother to learn the details of the Dawes Plan to cut reparations, stabilize Germany's currency, and insure payment of 2,500,000,000 marks—about $595,000,000— by the Germans to the Allies for World War I.

Americans were too busy making money and enjoying themselves to care anything about international affairs. Never before had the people felt so secure."

Anxious crowds throng the streets outside the New York Stock Exchange after the market collapsed on October 29, 1929. Called the worst day in the American stock market's history, it marked the beginning of the Great Depression.

dent Herbert Hoover gave tacit approval to the bankers' and brokers' actions. But in spite of all of the optimistic speeches, both government and business leaders knew by the fall of 1929 that a crash in the market was not only possible but probable. They had been afraid that talking about it would only start panic selling sooner. However, they could not postpone the inevitable.

The Crash

A downward trend started in September 1929 and continued steadily. And on October 29, 1929, Black Tuesday, the American stock market had its worst day in history. Although stock prices rose again briefly, and the economic collapse was spread out over several weeks, October 29 is viewed as the beginning of the Great Depression in the United States.

After the collapse of the stock market, more banks failed and were unable to give depositors the money from their accounts. As a result, people panicked and withdrew their money from those banks that were still in business. They began to hoard their money in mattresses, walls of their houses, tin cans buried in their yards—anywhere but in the banks. When people hoard money, they take it out of circulation. This

Jobless men enjoy a free meal at a Chicago soup kitchen in 1930. The ranks of the unemployed swelled as factories closed or were forced to lay off workers.

causes more banks to declare bankruptcy. When money is in a bank, it is available to be loaned out for construction, home-building, and other industries that create jobs and goods. Hoarding allows the supply of cash to dwindle and leads to the banks' closing because they have no cash to lend or to invest.

The October crash on Wall Street, America's financial center, was followed by the Great Depression. The crash alone did not cause the depression. Farmers were already in trouble and had never fully recovered from the recession of the early 1920s. European and American farmers continued to produce more food than consumers could use, so prices fell. With decreased profits, American farmers could not repay their mortgages. And European farmers could not purchase the products that American and Asian industries were trying to export. The new technology that had made each worker more productive not only decreased the number of people employed, but also increased the amount of goods produced. Because of farm troubles and unemployment, there were not enough consumers able to purchase all of those products. That resulted in more factories closing and more people becoming unemployed. The American banking system was not regulated, so no government agency was insuring that the investments that it made were sound, and because of bad investments, banks started to fail in large numbers. In a nation and world in which the economic decisions of one nation affected the prosperity of others, one failure and crisis led to another. But the mutual distrust that had followed World War I made international cooperation impossible. Now it was up to each nation to decide how to respond to this worldwide disaster.

2 Hoover and Roosevelt

In the United States the crash of the stock market and the ensuing economic depression precipitated, or provoked, a debate about the relationship between the government and the people. Before the crash Americans supported a strict separation between government and business. They believed that prosperity depended on limiting the government's influence on the economic system and opposed all forms of governmental regulation of industry, even if that resulted in unscrupulous banking practices or hazardous working conditions. People believed that freedom from government control was more important to the maintenance of democratic self-government, individual choice, and most importantly, economic progress than was preventing fraud and abuse. This philosophy was embodied in President Herbert Clark Hoover, who served during the first three years of the Great Depression.

A Self-Made Man

Herbert Hoover was a self-made millionaire who had easily been elected president in 1928, riding the tide of the economic prosperity of the 1920s, which he and his fellow Republicans took credit for. A for-

mer businessman with several international corporations, Hoover believed that American success and continued prosperity depended on limiting the government's influence on the economic system. In a speech delivered in New York City on October 22, 1928, Hoover expressed his philosophy on government interference in the economy:

President Herbert Hoover believed that limiting government interference in the economy was the key to ending the depression.

I have witnessed not only at home but abroad the many failures of government in business. I have seen its tyrannies, its injustices, its destruction of self-government, its undermining of the very instincts which carry our people forward to progress.[6]

Hoover maintained his convictions even after the Wall Street crash plunged the nation into the depression. He believed that, left to its own devices, business would solve the country's economic problems. Therefore, his first response to the events of October 1929 was to meet with business, labor, and agricultural leaders. Less than one month after the crash, at the Conference for Continued Industrial Progress, he asked them to voluntarily cooperate with each other to hold the line on wages and unemployment. He also appealed to the nation's governors to stimulate the economies in their states by hiring private companies to complete public works projects such as roads and buildings. The president optimistically predicted that the economic crisis would end in sixty days if businesspeople were allowed to solve their own problems in their own way.

But the crisis did not end in sixty days. Unemployment reached six million in 1930. Construction was down 25 percent, and building-trades officials in Chicago reported that 75 percent of their members were out of work. The number of unemployed workers reached eight million by 1931. There were food riots in New York in which hundreds of hungry men and

A Private, Not a Public, Solution

In this excerpt from his 1930 annual address to Congress, quoted in Harris Gaylord Warren's book Herbert Hoover and the Great Depression, *President Hoover stresses that the depression would be cured by the efforts of private industry and charities, not government involvement.*

"Economic depression cannot be cured by legislative action or executive pronouncement. Economic wounds must be healed by the action of the cells of the economic body—the producers and consumers themselves. Recovery can be expedited and its effects mitigated [relieved] by cooperative action. That cooperation requires that every individual should sustain faith and courage; that each should maintain his self-reliance; . . . that the vast majority whose income is unimpaired should not hoard out of fear but should seek to assist his neighbors who may be less fortunate; that each industry should assist its own employees; that each community and each State should assume its full responsibilities for organization of employment and relief of distress with that sturdiness and independence which built a great Nation."

By 1932, ten million people were out of work. Unable to pay their rents or mortgages, some people were forced to sleep on city streets and benches.

women marched into grocery stores and took food off the shelves. In T. H. Watkins's *The Great Depression*, one witness described a food riot in Minneapolis:

> On February 25, several hundred men and women smashed the windows of a grocery and meat market in Minneapolis and grabbed bacon and ham, fruit and canned goods. When one of the store owners drew a revolver, the crowd jumped him and broke his arm.[7]

Homeless people were sleeping on the streets of every major city, and their numbers were growing every day as middle-class families were evicted from their homes.

In October 1931 deposits in U.S. banks had decreased by six billion dollars as investors withdrew their funds and began hoarding money. Over ten million workers were unemployed that year.

No Government Help

During the Great Depression there were no governmental social agencies, welfare departments, or aid to dependent children services. The only assistance people could get was from churches and private charities like the Salvation Army. Even as unemployment continued to rise, Hoover refused to approve governmental financial assistance to the needy. He believed that private charities could meet the needs of all the poor. But churches and private charities could not provide for all of the depression-era poor. Middle-class people who had supported such organizations were no longer able to contribute because they had joined the ranks of the unemployed and needy themselves.

Times were especially bad for farmers, who were losing their farms in large numbers. A bushel of wheat was selling for thirty cents at the end of 1932, down from three dollars a bushel in 1920. In the conservative, law-abiding Midwest—the heartland of America—groups of farmers resisted sheriffs who were sent to auction off farms and threatened to hang judges who foreclosed on neighbors' farms. These acts of lawlessness brought fears of revolution to the entire country. Farmers pledged to stop shipping food to market unless they were paid enough to cover the expense of growing it.

Hoover continued to stand on principles that were rooted in noninterference in industry and in private charity, not public welfare. However, he was flexible enough to propose the establishment of the Reconstruction Finance Corporation (RFC), which would lend money to businesses, banks, and railroads to prevent them from declaring bankruptcy and increasing the unemployment rate. Most of the money was lent to big industries, not small businesspeople. According to a 1933 report on the Reconstruction Finance Corporation:

> 7.4% of the borrowers received 53.5% of the money loaned. Nor should it be forgotten that loans to small financial institutions generally went through them to the big-city banks. Thus R.F.C. funds generally filtered into the large centers; the R.F.C., instead of the large banks, became the creditor. Under the Republican administration, most of the loans went to small institutions but most of the money went to big institutions.[8]

In other words, large numbers of small businesses borrowed money, but they immediately handed it over to the few big

Hundreds of Brooklyn's needy line up for a free meal from a local charity. With no government assistance available for the needy, private charities and churches struggled to provide relief for the rapidly growing numbers of unemployed.

The Hawley-Smoot Tariff Act

In spite of his policy of not interfering with business, one of Hoover's first acts as president was to approve the Hawley-Smoot Tariff Act, which protected American businesses from foreign competition. In Herbert Hoover and the Great Depression, *author Harris Gaylord Warren writes:*

"The United States should have taken the lead in an effort to achieve multilateral [international] reduction of trade barriers. However doubtful prospects for success may have been, Hoover should have called for an international economic conference in 1930 and should have exercised his leadership to bring a drastic reduction of tariffs. Many noted economists had presented unanswerable arguments against Republican tariff policy, but the President had refused to heed them. Hoover often argued that the Depression orginated abroad; conditions abroad prevented recovery in the United States. Then why the emphasis on a unilateral tariff that could do nothing except worsen conditions abroad? Why not exercise the leadership necessary to bring about cooperation in eliminating those foreign sources of depression?"

banks to which they owed money. Therefore, the real winners were a few big bankers. As a result, the American people viewed the RFC as a relief program for big business at a time when there was no direct federal government relief for individuals.

Hoover established the President's Organization on Unemployment Relief to help private agencies distribute money and food to the poor. But the needs of the people were overwhelming. In 1932 the executive secretary of the American Association of Social Workers, Walter West, stated, "It is my conviction that there are no amounts in sight from public or private sources now which would come anywhere near meeting the necessary relief for the winter or for the next two years."[9]

Under political pressure from his own party and the Democrats, Hoover signed the Emergency Relief and Construction Act in July 1932. This act allowed the Reconstruction Finance Corporation to lend money to states for public projects that would provide jobs and food for the unemployed. In proposing that the RFC expand its operations, Hoover said:

I hold that the maintenance of the sense of individual and personal responsibility of men to their neighbors and the proper separation of functions of the Federal and local governments require the maintenance of the fundamental principle that the obligation of distress rests upon the individuals, upon the communities and upon the states. In order, however, that there may be no failure on the part of any state to meet its obligations in this direction I have, after consultation with some of the party leaders on both sides, favored authorization of the Reconstruction Finance Corporation to loan up to $300,000,000 to state governments.[10]

But even when writing his memoirs of the depression years, Hoover cited government statistics based on flawed studies on the infant mortality rate and causes of death to show that there was no need for government charity. Although starvation contributed to deaths by affecting the body's immune system and making people more susceptible to diseases such as pneumonia, disease, not starvation, was listed as the cause of death. Hoover used those statistics to maintain that people were not starving. He stated that the records of the United States Public Health Service "not only proved that there was no widespread undernourishment, but also that the solic-itude [care] for those in difficulty by the 3,000 local volunteer committees of admirable men and women was having magnificent results."[11]

This reliance on statistics that clearly contradicted what people saw in their cities and neighborhoods led Americans to distrust the motives of the Hoover administration. As they entered the third year of the depression, the unemployed needed to feel that their president cared about the fact that they were homeless and taking food from garbage cans. Forty-five percent of factory workers were still unemployed. There were hunger marches in major cities as families struggled to live on $3.15 worth of food a week. Over 180,000 impoverished families in New York received no relief at all because public and private charities had run out of funds. Government advice to plant a garden and grow their own food was of little use to city dwellers trapped in tenements.

Marchers in Boston demand government assistance for the unemployed, protesting what they see as a lack of government sympathy for their plight.

Hoover's Popularity Plunges

Through it all Hoover remained certain that if America stayed on course, private industry would improve, thereby decreasing unemployment and poverty. He wanted four more years in the White House to prove that his policies of nonintervention would result in economic recovery. No one contested his nomination at the 1932 Republican national convention, because to challenge and reject Hoover and his philosophy would require Republicans to accept some of the blame for the depression.

Heading into the campaign season, Hoover's secretary of war, Patrick J. Hurley, proclaimed, "Basically, the question before the American people today is individualism against some form of collectivism."[12] In spite of the lack of economic progress, Americans were afraid that government control of the economy would result in the cancellation of individual freedom and rights. Hoover's campaign strategy, therefore, was to tell Americans that things would get worse if the government interfered in the economic crisis: "Let no man tell you it could not be worse. It could be so much worse that these days now, distressing as they are, would look like veritable prosperity."[13]

As they had throughout Hoover's term, Hoover and the Republican Party underestimated the extent to which the people were not just in distress, but in real pain and willing to try something new. Historian Robert S. McElvaine believes that Hoover's primary contribution was that he tried to place the burden of recovery on the voluntary actions of private industry and private charities. In the face of continued economic problems, Americans became willing to accept more government involvement in the economy:

> Hoover's voluntary cooperation opened the way for the New Deal's government-directed plans. Before people will accept what they see as extreme programs, moderate ones must be shown to be insufficient. This was one of Hoover's chief contributions. Thanks to his efforts, no one could justly complain (although of course many protested without good cause) that the government intervened without giving the private sector a chance to recover on its own.[14]

A Different Philosophy

Franklin Delano Roosevelt (FDR), the Democratic nominee for the presidency in 1932, recognized the severity and depth of the economic crisis and was willing to try new, and some said extreme, programs. Roosevelt was a member of a wealthy New York family whose life had been one of luxury and privilege. He had made public service his career, serving first as assistant secretary of the navy and later as governor of New York. But the experience that most profoundly affected his life was his struggle with polio, an infectious virus that attacks the spinal column and nervous system. Paralyzed as a result of this disease, he wore metal braces and used a cane. When not in public, he used a wheelchair. The illness had not only changed him physically; it influenced his politics as well. He became interested in alleviating the problems and sufferings of others.

In his acceptance speech at the Democratic national convention in July 1932, Roosevelt outlined the basic premise of his program. He wanted to eliminate waste in government and make the federal government solvent. He wanted to regulate the banking and investment industries by making them prove that their investments were safe and not based on speculation. To give jobs to more people, he wanted to shorten the workday and workweek. Lastly, he wanted to initiate public works and conservation projects, and to repeal protective tariffs that limited trade. Roosevelt declared:

> Ours must be a party of liberal thought, of planned action, of enlightened international outlook, and of the

Franklin Delano Roosevelt was elected president in 1932 with a promise of "a new deal for the American people."

greatest good to the greatest number of our citizens. . . . I pledge you, I pledge myself, to a new deal for the American people.[15]

After his election the term *New Deal* would be applied to the various acts which made up his program.

The idea that government should be actively involved in relieving economic hardship was revolutionary. As governor of New York, Roosevelt had used National Guard armories to house homeless people, formed a commission to study the concept of unemployment insurance, and established the Temporary Emergency Relief Administration to fund public works jobs for unemployed citizens of New York State. It was this progressive government involvement in the lives of the people that had brought Roosevelt to national attention and, eventually, the Democratic nomination for the presidency.

As for his opponent, in the weeks preceding the election, Herbert Hoover was so unpopular that it was unsafe for him to leave the safety of the White House to campaign. The election-night results, therefore, were not surprising. Roosevelt received 22,809,638 votes to Hoover's 15,758,901. He won a majority of the votes in forty-two states and won the electoral college by 472 to 59 votes.

FDR Takes Charge

On Saturday, March 4, 1933, Franklin Delano Roosevelt took the oath of office as the thirty-second president of the United States. In his inaugural address he tried to calm the anxiety of the people as he declared:

Depositors crowd around the American Union Bank in New York City after it failed. President Roosevelt declared a federal bank holiday in order to prevent depositors from removing more money from the banks, and to stop further escalation of the bank crisis.

This great Nation will endure as it has endured, will revive and prosper. So, first of all, let me assert my firm belief that the only thing that we have to fear is fear itself—nameless, unreasoning, unjustified terror which paralyzes needed efforts to convert retreat into advance.[16]

President Roosevelt took immediate action. He called for a special session of Congress to meet on March 9. Then he declared a federal bank holiday to temporarily close all of the banks in America until further notice.

This action prevented depositors from removing more money from the banks and gave government inspectors time to examine the records of all banks so that they could determine which banks were solvent. Banks that were unsound remained closed until they proved to bank auditors that they could remain solvent after reopening. Those that had been solvent were allowed to reopen immediately after the bank holiday. And because only solvent banks would be allowed to reopen, the people were encouraged to have a renewed confidence in the banks.

He then called on a group of bankers to determine the most effective way to give depositors access to their money. Secretary of the Treasury William H. Woodin wanted the federal government to take advantage of the Federal Reserve Act to print more money, which could then be loaned to banks to make sure they had enough currency on hand. But currency must be backed up by a valuable commodity, or economic good, and there was not enough gold bullion in the Treasury to back up the new money. This was partially due to the fact that when the economy began to be sour, investors had demanded

The First Fireside Chat

In his first fireside chat, excerpted from his book Nothing to Fear, *President Franklin D. Roosevelt explained the government's response to the banking crisis in terms that ordinary citizens could easily understand.*

"My friends,

I want to talk for a few minutes with the people of the United States about banking. . . . I know that when you understand what we in Washington have been about, I shall continue to have your cooperation. . . . I issued the proclamation providing for the nationwide bank holiday, and this was the first step in the Government's reconstruction of our financial and economic fabric. The second step was the legislation promptly and patriotically passed by the Congress confirming my proclamation and broadening my powers so that it became possible in view of the requirement of time to extend the holiday and lift the ban of that holiday gradually. This law also gave authority to develop a program of rehabilitation of our banking facilities. . . . The third stage has been the series of regulations permitting the banks to continue their functions."

FDR appeals to the American public via radio during one of his famous fireside chats.

the gold which backed their savings and had been hoarding it. To encourage people to redeposit the gold that they had been hoarding, the Federal Reserve Board declared that if people did not redeposit the gold, their names would be published the following Monday when the banks opened. Fearing reprisals, thousands of people redeposited their gold, enabling the government to print more money.

When Congress convened on Thursday, March 9, it immediately passed the Emergency Banking Act. Less than an hour later President Roosevelt signed it into law. This act of Congress gave the president the sole power to control all economic transactions with other countries and the flow of gold and currency out of the country. It also allowed banks to sell their stock to the government's Reconstruction Finance Corporation to obtain money. The act formally approved the bank holiday and extended it by three days to give government examiners sufficient time to examine the records of all of the banks. As a result, only banks that had enough money to back their deposits were able to reopen.

The Fireside Chats

While bank examiners determined which banks could reopen on March 13, the president went to work to make sure that the American public would make deposits in those banks, not withdraw more money. Radio broadcasts had been used by presidents before Roosevelt, but these had been formal speeches delivered to large audiences. Such speeches often came across as insincere. Roosevelt, however, understood that the power of this relatively new medium was in the intimacy it created between the speaker and the listener. He realized that the radio brought him into people's homes as their guest. Therefore, he planned to speak in a friendly, conversational tone. He wanted the people to feel that he was sitting in their living rooms, in front of their fireplaces, having a chat with them.

During that first "fireside chat" on March 12, Roosevelt attempted to describe the banking crisis in terms the average American could understand and to explain how the bank holiday and the Emergency Banking Act would insure that only solvent banks would reopen and that people's money would be safe in banks. He concluded by saying, "I can assure you that it is safer to keep your money in a reopened bank than under a mattress."[17] Then Roosevelt waited to see if the people believed him.

Roosevelt's first fireside chat was broadcast on 150 stations and reached an audience of sixty million Americans. Small investors listened to him, and, more importantly for the success of his program, they believed him. When the banks opened on Monday, March 13, the amount of deposits exceeded that of withdrawals. And by the end of the month, $1.2 billion had been redeposited in America's banks.

Because of its success, the March 12 broadcast was just the first of many fireside chats that the president would have with the people. The fireside chats were "Franklin Roosevelt speaking to the people, and the people understood exactly what he was saying. FDR learned the art of making political issues understandable."[18]

This overwhelming vote of confidence in government intervention in the economy gave the new president an advantage in dealing with Congress. The public's response showed that many Americans wanted the government to offer them some protection from the actions of businesspeople and the risks of the marketplace. The special session of Congress stretched from March 9 until June 15, exactly one hundred days after it had been convened and has become known as the Hundred Days. Roosevelt presented and won approval for the programs that he believed would lift America out of the depression. Those programs combined would become known as the New Deal.

3 The First Hundred Days

The Emergency Banking Act, which had resolved the banking crisis, was only the first of the major acts that composed the New Deal legislation. During the first one hundred days of his presidency, Roosevelt used the public's confidence in him to get Congress to approve more acts and programs to alleviate suffering and improve the economy.

The second of those acts was the Economy Act. During his first week in office, FDR met with budget director Lewis Douglas, who had been given the task of recommending spending cuts. Roosevelt wanted to make a good-faith effort to cut his administration's spending to try to reduce the federal debt of almost three billion dollars. Also called the Bill to Maintain the Credit of the United States, the act was supposed to reduce the debt. The act lowered all government salaries and pensions by 15 percent, eliminated health benefits to veterans whose illnesses were unrelated to wartime service, and eliminated nonessential government activities, such as scientific research. The Economy Act reorganized the federal government by consolidating departments to reduce waste, cut bureaucracy, and eliminate duplication. It may seem ironic that one of the first acts of the New Deal was to reduce the budget, since New Deal pro-

grams would eventually spend billions of dollars to provide relief and revive the American economy, increasing the federal deficit (the amount spent and owed by the government) in the process. But Roosevelt did believe that balancing the budget was an important step in full recovery.

Through a third act, Roosevelt established the Civilian Conservation Corps (CCC). The CCC, under the jurisdiction of the Departments of Labor, Agriculture, War, and the Interior, paid young men thirty dollars a month and provided food, clothing, and shelter in exchange for their work in the nation's forests and parks. One of the longest lasting of the New Deal programs, it helped two and a half million young men to survive the depression and continued until 1943, when unemployed young men were needed in the armed forces.

Relieving Farmers' Plight

Roosevelt also attempted to alleviate the problems of farmers. In January 1933 Edward A. O'Neal, president of the independent American Farm Bureau Federation, had told a Senate committee, "Unless something is done for the American

A poster encourages young men to join the Civilian Conservation Corps. This successful New Deal program provided two and a half million much-needed jobs.

ton, wheat, tobacco, corn, or hogs, it had to be approved in a national referendum by a majority of the farmers who produced those products. This was necessary to make sure that the controls reflected regional needs and were not simply being imposed on farmers by federal agents. Local committees of farmers would be responsible for checking the farms in their areas for compliance. The money to pay for the program would come not from the Treasury, but from a tax on the industries that processed the crops: the canning plants, millers, meat packers, and textile manufacturers.

At the same time, the Emergency Farm Mortgage Act allowed farmers to refinance their mortgages at lower rates. This act was so popular that it was attached to the Agricultural Adjustment Act in an effort to pressure Congress into voting for it. Both the Agricultural Adjustment Act, which created the Agricultural Adjustment Administration, and the Emergency Farm Mortgage Act were signed into law on May 12, 1933. Writing about that time, Rexford G. Tugwell, one of FDR's agricultural advisers, noted:

farmer we will have a revolution within twelve months."[19]

Roosevelt's Agricultural Adjustment Act proposed in March 1933 was heavily influenced by fifty farm leaders and farming experts. They had been invited to Washington to work with the Department of Agriculture to formulate a plan to help farmers avoid bankruptcy and start making profits again. The basic principle of the bill was to raise farm prices by paying farmers to produce less. However, before such control programs would be put into effect for particular products, such as cot-

To the critics it seemed ridiculous to pay farmers for not planting crops. They pointed out that the production of food was being limited at a time when many people were hungry. They did not listen when the answer was made that staple crops existed in huge surpluses at give-away prices—and still were not in demand. Even if the nation had been prosperous, wheat and cotton in the quantities being produced would not be used or needed. What was needed was meat, dairy products, and other protein foods, and the production of these was being encouraged, not limited. The program was popular with farmers, however, who understood from hard experience how important the parity [equality] concept was. They cooperated fully.[20]

The Tennessee Valley Authority

A major problem in expanding industrial development and providing job opportunities in the South was the lack of inexpensive and reliable electrical power throughout the area. To bring electricity to the farms and rural communities of the South, Roosevelt proposed the establish-ment of the Tennessee Valley Authority (TVA) to harness the power of the Tennessee River. However, in proposing the legislation, Roosevelt envisioned an even greater impact on the area than just the introduction of electrical power. He hoped that this action would improve conservation in the area, especially of the floodplains that some were attempting to farm, and open the South to modern industrial development. He referred to the successful Muscle Shoals hydroelectric project that had been developed during World War I and said:

> It is clear that the [Muscle] Shoals development is but a small part of the usefulness of the entire Tennessee River. Such use, if envisioned in its en-

The Tennessee Valley Authority installs a generator at Wheeler Dam that is designed to harness the power of the Tennessee River. The TVA succeeded in bringing electricity to southern regions that had previously been without power.

The Arrival of the New Dealers

One of the administration's primary goals was to provide jobs. And with the establishment of so many new government agencies, many of those jobs were with the government in Washington. In The Great Depression, *Robert S. McElvaine writes about those New Dealers.*

"Despite the important roles played by several Cabinet officers, it was not the department heads who gave the New Deal its special spirit. As Franklin Roosevelt almost instantly turned the federal government into the center of activity in a depressed nation, thousands of ambitious and idealistic young men—and some women—flocked to Washington. It was that rarest of times when ambition and idealism could go hand in hand. These were the 'New Dealers,' the seemingly tireless young people of ideas who were bent upon changing the world and being part of the most dramatic transformation in their nation's history. . . . An 'anything can be done' spirit—diametrically [completely] opposed to that of the later Hoover administration—took over. Many New Dealers wore their hair far longer than was the style not through any desire to display nonconformity, but because they did not take the time to get haircuts; so much of more importance had to be done. Even festive occasions turned into serious discussions of social and economic problems and how best to solve them. 'It's exciting and educational to be alive and in Washington these days,' one young man wrote several months after the start of the New Deal."

tirety, transcends mere power development; it enters the wide fields of flood control, soil erosion, afforestation [establishing new forests], elimination from agricultural use of marginal lands, and distribution and diversification of industry.[21]

The effects of the legislation that created the Tennessee Valley Authority were more far-reaching than had been envisioned by the most progressive of its sup-

porters. Established by law on May 18, 1933, the TVA involved the most extensive federal involvement in regional planning in American history. The TVA did not just develop hydroelectric plants on the Tennessee River to produce power. The cost of producing this power was then used as a standard by which private power rates could be determined. It provided electricity for farm areas that had been without power and made industry feasible for the area. The dams were also used for flood control, and conservation programs re-claimed soil that had been damaged by generations of inefficient farming. In addition, the educational programs provided by the TVA were designed to enable the region's impoverished local residents to become more efficient farmers and skilled industrial workers.

In his analysis of New Deal programs, Professor Paul K. Conkin wrote, "Of all the early New Deal programs, the Tennessee Valley Authority . . . was the most imaginative in conception and one of the most successful in operation."[22]

Hundreds of hungry people line up for a one cent meal. Assistance like this became scarcer as the depression worsened.

Supplementing Charity

The Federal Emergency Relief Administration (FERA) was designed to alleviate some of the suffering caused by the difficult economic times. Under the Hoover administration private charities and local governmental agencies had borne the brunt of the responsibility for aiding the poor. But by 1932 private charities were so overburdened that they were unable to help most of the needy. Federal and state spending for charitable purposes was $1.67 a person annually on a national average. These efforts were inadequate, so Roosevelt asked Congress for funds that could be given to the states for relief. As his adviser, Rexford Tugwell, noted in his memoir of those days:

> This was the acceptance of responsibility for the welfare of individuals that he had promised. To draw unemployment benefits from the U.S. Treasury still seemed horrifying to most Republicans—and to some Democrats. But this was what the election had all been about. The President was simply carrying out what he regarded as a commitment to those who had elected him.[23]

Signed into law on May 12, 1933, the Federal Emergency Relief Act authorized $500 million in grants to the states and created the Federal Emergency Relief Administration to organize the distribution of those funds. Harry Hopkins, the director of relief services in New York State, was named as the administrator. He understood the urgency of the problem. An economist once told Hopkins that there was no need for FERA because, in the long run, the economy would provide jobs

The CWA

Hank Oettinger worked as a printer during the Great Depression. In Studs Terkel's Hard Times, *Oettinger remembered the public's first reaction to the Civil Works Administration.*

"I can remember the first week of the C.W.A. checks. It was on a Friday. That night everybody had gotten his check. The first check a lot of them had in three years. Everybody was out celebrating. It was like a festival in some old European city. . . . I never saw such a change in attitude. Instead of walking around feeling dreary and looking sorrowful, everybody was joyous. Like a feast day. They were toasting each other. They had money in their pockets for the first time."

for people. Hopkins replied, "People don't eat in the long run, they have to eat every day."[24]

However, many employed Americans continued to oppose giving relief directly to individuals. They feared that giving people money instead of jobs would destroy the work ethic and our economic system. Both Harry Hopkins and the president understood this concern. Hopkins agreed

> that direct relief took from people "their sense of independence and their sense of individual destiny.". . . Giving a person something to do in exchange for his check "preserved a man's morale," Hopkins contended. "It gives him a chance to do something socially useful."[25]

Therefore, one of Hopkins's first acts was to set up a temporary work program for the winter of 1933–1934: the Civil Works Administration (CWA). That winter four million workers were hired at a rate of fifteen dollars a week. That does not seem like much money. However, at a time when

two-thirds of Americans had incomes of less than twenty-five hundred dollars a year, fifteen dollars a week was considered a fair wage for CWA projects. But the fact that it was more than twice the amount they would receive from a relief check without working provided an incentive to work. Hopkins was always more interested in getting money into people's pockets so they could afford food and shelter than in the actual usefulness or quality of the work provided. As a result, the CWA, which had provided jobs like shoveling snow off city streets or raking leaves in the parks, came under a great deal of criticism. Although the Federal Emergency Relief Administration continued to operate throughout the depression, the Civil Works Administration was eliminated after that first winter. The president was worried that people were becoming dependent on these jobs instead of looking for jobs in private industry, jobs that could strengthen the economy.

After all, strengthening the economy through the development of jobs in private industry and creating a strong agricultural

Workers demonstrate in New York City's Union Square for continuation of the CWA program. FDR eliminated the Civil Works Administration because he wanted to encourage people to seek jobs in private industry.

system were still the primary goals. Having successfully proposed legislation to alleviate suffering and to address the crises in banking and agriculture, the administration would have been content to wait until the next regular session of Congress to develop and introduce its plan for industrial recovery. However, events in the Senate forced the Roosevelt administration to act immediately.

The Thirty-Hour Bill

In early April the Senate approved legislation introduced by Senator Hugo Black of Alabama and supported by the large labor union, the American Federation of Labor.

The Black bill stated that products made by workers who had been required to work more than a six-hour day or a five-day week could not be sold or transported across state lines. Nicknamed the Thirty-Hour Bill, it was expected to pass the House as well. Labor leaders had been urging industrial reform for years to combat poor working conditions in many industries. The workweek in some industries had risen to seventy hours, and many workers earned only pennies an hour. There had been an increase in the use of child labor in factories, and unsafe working conditions were common.

Although he understood the need for reform, Roosevelt opposed the Black bill because it set rigid limits for maximum hours but failed to mention a minimum wage. That was a vital component if people were to live decently on what they could earn during those thirty hours. He was faced with a dilemma. He did not want to sign the bill, but he did not want to veto any recovery bill or give Congress the opportunity to oppose him by overriding one of his vetoes.

As a result of all of this pressure for industrial reform, Roosevelt appointed a committee to design a recovery plan that would be acceptable to business, labor, and government. The result was the National Industrial Recovery Act. The act was an attempt to plan our economic system more carefully by encouraging industry to produce only as much as consumers could afford to purchase. In reality, the act was a confusing composite of both probusiness and prolabor philosophies. According to

depression-era historian Robert McElvaine, the legislation simply reflected the conflict within American society between desires for individualism and efficiency: "Our ideal is individualism, but we covet the efficiency and comfort provided by large organization."[26]

The National Industrial Recovery Act, signed into law on June 16, 1933, created the National Recovery Administration (NRA). This act benefited both the owners of factories and the workers in those factories. It allowed industries that normally would have competed with each other to work together to determine how much of a product each would produce and to agree on a set price for the product. Industries were willing to do that because, under the current economic conditions, surpluses of products resulted in

The government's purpose for creating the NRA—to benefit both factory owners and workers—is depicted in this 1933 cartoon.

prices so low that companies could not make profits. It also guaranteed labor's right to organize and to form unions in those industries, eliminated the employment of children under the age of sixteen in factories, and provided workers with a forty-hour workweek, a minimum wage of thirty cents an hour, and safer working conditions. A separate section of the act established the Public Works Administration (PWA) to replace the Civil Works Administration and put the unemployed to work on long-range government projects.

General Hugh S. Johnson, who was appointed administrator, had a definite flair for public relations and the dramatic. Industries that had agreed to take part in the act displayed blue eagles and the motto "We Do Our Part." There were parades and rallies in many cities. And songs proclaimed:

Join the good old N.R.A., Boys, and we
  will end this awful strife.
Join it with the spirit that will give the
  eagle life.
Join it, folks, then push and pull, many
  millions strong,
While we go marching to Prosperity.[27]

Although sections of the legislation had long-term implications, overall it did not contribute to economic recovery. Businessmen did not cooperate. As soon as the law passed, factories increased production to take advantage of cheap labor before the forty-hour week and minimum wage provisions took effect. As soon as inventories were built up, there were layoffs and an increase in unemployment. Higher prices went into effect because of less competition among businesses.

In terms of immediate economic recovery, the most effective section of the

---

CWA Success

Lorena Hickok traveled around America, reporting to Harry Hopkins, chief of FERA and CWA, on the efforts of the Federal Emergency Relief Administration. This 1933 entry is recorded in Richard Lowitt and Maurine Beasley's One Third of a Nation.

"Something over 5,000 men, who went to work with picks and shovels and wheelbarrows last Monday morning, lined up and got paid—MONEY. It was for only half a week's work. The payrolls were made up Thursday night, but for many, many of them it was the first money they'd seen in months. They took it with wide grins and made beelines for the grocery stores, NOT to shove a grocery order across the counter but to go where they pleased and buy what they pleased, with cash. And along about a week from today these and many thousands more will be dropping into drygoods stores, too, and clothing stores. I wonder if you have any idea of what CWA is doing for the morale of these people and the communities."

PWA workers begin construction on Boulder Dam in 1933. The Public Works Administration's large-scale construction projects created many new jobs for skilled workers.

National Industrial Recovery Act was the establishment of the Public Works Administration, which was created to organize federally sponsored projects that could hire the unemployed and give them work rather than charity. Under the direction of Harold Ickes, the secretary of the interior, the Public Works Administration focused on long-term, carefully planned construction projects, not on immediate employment. It put one billion dollars into the economy to pay for materials, architects, engineers, and skilled construction workers. The PWA produced the causeway from mainland Florida to Key West, the Grand Coulee Dam in Washington State, Boulder Dam, now Hoover Dam, across the Colorado River, thousands of schools and hospitals, and New York City's Triborough Bridge. It was one of the most successful of the New Deal programs.

Mixed Reactions to Regulating Business

The same could not be said for the National Recovery Act as a whole. The act had tried to reconcile America's desire for both individualism and industrial efficiency, and it failed because it could not provide both. Many consumers resented the freedom it gave to big business to set prices. On the other hand, others felt that it was un-American to regulate business at all. Congress had given the NRA a two-year life span. It probably would have died naturally if the Supreme Court had not killed it. On May 27, 1935, in the case of *Schechter Poultry v. United States*, the act was declared unconstitutional and became invalid. In that case the owners of the Schechter Poultry Company in New York claimed that the

Remembering the CCC

Blackie Gold, a former member of the Civilian Conservation Corps, told Studs Terkel about his reasons for joining the CCC and the work he did. This excerpt is from Terkel's book Hard Times.

"We had to go out and beg for coal, buy bread that's two, three days old. My dad died when I was an infant. I went to an orphan home for fellas. Stood [stayed] there till I was seventeen years old. I came out into the big wide world, and my mother who was trying to raise my six older brothers and sisters, couldn't afford another mouth to feed. So I enlisted in the Civilian Conservation Corps. . . . Those big trees you see along the highways— all these big forests was all built by the CCC. We went along plain, barren ground. There were no trees. We just dug trenches and kept planting trees. You could plant about a hundred an hour."

The CCC provided job opportunities for young men in the nation's forests and parks. In exchange for their labor, the young men received food, clothing, shelter, and a monthly salary of thirty dollars.

federal government had no right to regulate the working conditions or wages of their workers and the price of their product because their business was operated within the state of New York. The Supreme Court agreed that the NRA violated states' rights, and the act was declared invalid.

The domestic economy had been the Roosevelt administration's primary focus during the Hundred Days. The banking crisis had been resolved, with the result that banks were no longer closing, and Americans felt safe putting their money in banks. The Civilian Conservation Corps, the Agricultural Adjustment Administration, the Tennessee Valley Authority, the Federal Emergency Relief Administration, and the National Recovery Administration had been established. The president turned his attention to the international scene and the June 1933 World Economic Conference in London, a summit of economic leaders from the United States, Great Britain, France, and the rest of Europe to address the crisis of the worldwide depression.

The Hoover administration had committed the United States to attending because Herbert Hoover thought the root causes of America's depression were in Europe. Hoover wanted to use the conference to negotiate policies that would ultimately benefit the U.S. economy. The goal of the European nations at the conference was to stabilize their currencies and set definite exchange rates.

Roosevelt disagreed with the conference's emphasis on fixing rates of exchange. He declared, "The sound internal economic system of a nation is a greater factor in its well-being than the price of its currency in changing terms of the currencies of other nations."[28]

To that end, Roosevelt believed that the purpose of the conference should be to raise prices on agricultural and industrial commodities and give economic relief to nations that owed money in order to allow them to purchase more goods. He did not want to commit himself to an international plan of cooperation because it would severely limit his freedom to influence the American economy and to employ his New Deal programs. Those programs were based on governmental spending that would increase the U.S. deficit and affect the exchange rate between the dollar and other currencies. Therefore, he refused to approve the European proposals to stabilize the exchange rates; without American support, the World Economic Conference failed.

Americans generally approved of Roosevelt's stand. Ernest K. Lindley of the *New York Herald Tribune* wrote, "The United States has a President whose first regard is the national interest."[29] However, international reaction was shock and anger. Some economists, including Great Britain's John Maynard Keynes, said that Roosevelt was right, but the overall response was outrage and a feeling that the United States had betrayed the other industrial nations.

Although, in his acceptance speech at the 1932 Democratic national convention, Roosevelt had spoken of the need for an enlightened international outlook, national affairs were clearly the first priority of the New Deal. By failing to support the proposals of the World Economic Conference, the United States made it obvious that it would once again isolate itself from the world scene in order to solve its own problems in its own way.

4 A New Deal on the Farm and in the City

In spite of the quick action taken by the Roosevelt administration during the Hundred Days and the New Deal legislation, full economic recovery would eventually take almost ten years to be realized. Therefore, throughout the 1930s either the problems of unemployment and poverty or the fear of becoming impoverished affected every American family. "The Depression was a way of life for me, from the time I was twenty to the time I was thirty," Chicago schoolteacher Elsa Ponselle remembered. "I thought it was going to be forever and ever and ever. That people would always live in fear of losing their jobs. You know, *fear.*"[30]

The enormous diversity of the United States contributed to the difficulty in designing programs and policies to relieve the poverty that pervaded the nation throughout the decade of the 1930s. Fifty percent of Americans lived below the poverty level on family incomes of less than fifteen hundred dollars a year. One-

A poor Iowa family dines on the few meager scraps of food that comprise their Christmas dinner. During the depression, more than half of all American families had to scrape by on less than fifteen hundred dollars a year.

third of the nation had subsistence incomes of between fifteen hundred and twenty-five hundred dollars a year. Thus, the majority of Americans did not have enough food to eat or adequate places to live. It was not just a rural problem or an inner-city problem. There was poverty in both small towns and big cities from Maine to California. It was not just a black problem or a white problem or an immigrant problem. It affected people of every race and religion. Employment problems were not restricted to men or women, nor to the young or old. All of the people were either unemployed or living in fear that they would soon be unemployed. Although everyone was affected by the depression, their concerns and hardships were different, and New Deal programs and policies had to address the needs of all groups.

Middle Class Hard Hit

The Great Depression was the first economic recession to severely affect the middle class: the grocers, doctors, lawyers, teachers, and other professionals who lived in small towns and cities throughout America and the farmers of the South and Midwest. This was the group that lost its savings when the banks went bankrupt. And when their customers and patients and clients lost their jobs, their own businesses failed. First they lost their livelihoods, then they lost their homes. Because of the large numbers of people looking for work, employers were able to offer slave wages. Secretaries who earned fifty dollars a week before the depression were now accepting jobs at ten dollars.

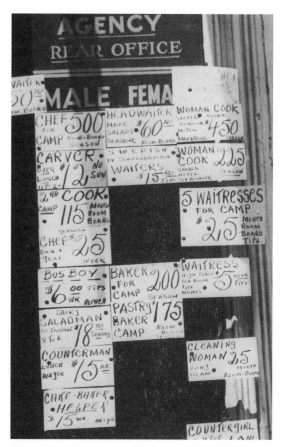

An employment agency advertises jobs available at substandard wages. Employers slashed wages as the increasing number of people seeking jobs made positions easy to fill.

Domestic workers accepted jobs for ten dollars a month. Skilled factory workers were reduced to twenty-five cents an hour, sometimes less. Because of the lack of new construction, architects and engineers could not find work. Many cities declared bankruptcy and could not pay their teachers, firefighters, and police. One news reporter wrote, "We saw a crowd of some fifty men fighting over a barrel of garbage which had been set outside the back door of a restaurant. American citizens fighting for scraps of food like animals!"[31] In an interview with presidential adviser Lorena Hickok, one woman explained:

> You just can't know what it's like to have to move your family out of the nice house you had in the suburbs, part paid for, down into an apartment, down into another apartment, smaller and in a worse neighborhood, down, down, down, until finally you end up in the slums.[32]

Depression-era living conditions made a lasting impression on the children. Another survivor recalled:

> I remember all of a sudden we had to move. My father lost his job and we moved into a double garage. The landlord didn't charge us rent for seven years. We had a coal stove, and we had to each take turns, the three of us kids, to warm our legs. It was awfully cold when you opened those garage doors. We would sleep with rugs and blankets over the top of us. Dress under the sheets.[33]

A factory worker's son recalled:

> Well, we lost our car and our house and kept moving from one house to another. Bill collectors hunted us down and came in droves. Every now and then my brother or Dad would find some sort of odd little something. Then we'd go wild. I mean we'd go wild over food. We'd eat until we were sick.[34]

Stubborn Pockets of Poverty

In spite of the New Deal's efforts to alleviate the people's suffering, many continued to be impoverished. The situation was especially critical in rural areas, where there were few charitable or government

On the Soup Line

In Hard Times, *Peggy Terry told Studs Terkel about her Oklahoma childhood during the depression.*

"I first noticed the difference when we'd come home from school in the evening. My mother'd send us to the soup line. And we were never allowed to cuss. If you happened to be one of the first ones in line, you didn't get anything but water that was on top. So we'd ask the guy that was ladling out the soup in the bucket to please dip down to get some meat and potatoes from the bottom of the kettle. But he wouldn't do it. . . . Then we'd go across the street. One place had bread, large loaves of bread. Down the road just a little piece was a big shed, and they gave milk. My sister and me would take two buckets each. And that's what we lived off for the longest time."

organizations to assist. With the loss of markets for their goods and the bank foreclosures on their property, farmers had been the first group to feel the effects of the economic crisis, and their problems would prove to be the most difficult to solve. The economy and the weather seemed to conspire during the 1930s to make life difficult for farmers. That was especially true of the southern tenant farmers and sharecroppers.

In the 1930s there were eight and a half million tenant farmers and sharecroppers living in the South, about half of whom were black. They rented the land that they farmed and repaid the landlord, or owner of the farmland, by giving him part of their crops. Tenant farmers were required to return 25 percent of their crops to the landlords; sharecroppers owed 50 percent of their crops. As part of the arrangement the tenants and sharecroppers had to purchase seeds and other farming materials, as well as their food, from a store owned by the landlord. At the end of the season, the landlord assessed the produce and subtracted what he was owed. The remainder was the tenant's profit for a year's work. Most earned less than two hundred dollars a year. At the end of the season, it was possible for some to owe their entire crop to the landlord and make no profit on it at all. Or they might even be in debt to the landlord and be forced to stay on the land until the debt was paid. It was a difficult and unprofitable life. One family of sharecroppers described their situation to members of the Federal Writers' Project:

The income from the crop is all we got to look to. Mr. Makepeace [the landowner] don't furnish us so much money a week like some landlords. He's got a store, and we go there and get what we need. He don't complain about our account, but books [notes] it as we buy. We've done had our settlement with him this year; our account was $375, which included our food and fertilizer and the labor for pickin' peas. We liked $220 payin' out. So we've got to start out the new year with that debt starin' at us. . . . We own our own team, two mules, our wagon and plows; Mr. Makepeace pays the fertilizer bill, but the expenses of the peanut machine and labor has to come out of us, for our part and Mr. Makepeace's too.[35]

After the passage of the Agricultural Adjustment Act, the tenant farmers' lives

A black tenant farmer in North Carolina. Many tenant farmers and sharecroppers were taken advantage of by greedy landlords.

became even tougher. Landowners were paid to destroy a percentage of their cotton, wheat, and tobacco crops and to slaughter their hogs. Many accepted the payment and destroyed the crops of their tenant farmers, but they failed to share the payment with the farmers. As a result, two and a half million tenant farmers and sharecroppers were evicted from the land and pushed even deeper into poverty. Landowners freely admitted that the act worked in their favor. One explained:

> In '34 I had I reckon four renters and I didn't make anything. I bought tractors on the money the government give me and got shed [rid] o' my renters. You find it everywhere all over the country that way. I did everything the government said—except keep my renters. The renters have been having it this way ever since the government come in.[36]

In response to this action Norman Thomas of the Socialist Party tried to organize both black and white sharecroppers to fight for their rights. The Southern Tenant Farmers Union was formed in Arkansas in the fall of 1934. Landowners reacted by evicting all those suspected of union activities. The leaders of the union met with the secretary of agriculture, Henry A. Wallace, to ask for his help in getting a fair deal for the tenants and sharecroppers. Wallace, however, took the side of the landowners. Cynics said that the administration's action was based on the fact that landowners voted but sharecroppers did not because they could not afford to pay the required poll tax. As a result, the tenants became more aggressive and militant, adding to the fear of worker unrest throughout the country.

The Beginnings of Violence

The following year the Southern Tenant Farmers Union went on strike at cotton-picking time. After ten days the landlords gave in and raised wages. But the truce lasted only long enough to get the landowners through the harvest season. As soon as it was over, they began to terrorize and evict those tenants and sharecroppers who were active in the union, increasing the number of displaced farmworkers in America.

Displaced tenant farmers and sharecroppers composed only one portion of the rural poor. Midwestern farmers were affected by another phenomenon that devastated their livelihoods: the dust bowl. Farmers in the Midwest had turned the grazing lands that stretched from the Dakotas to Oklahoma and Texas into farmland by using newly developed motorized tractors. They dug up the tough prairie sod that had conserved moisture in that dry region. At the time it seemed like a good use of formerly unproductive land. But then, starting in 1933, a series of droughts hit the area. When the wind swept over the plains, it gathered up the dry soil and buried the area in a blizzard of dust. The worst of the dust storms occurred from the Texas panhandle north to the Dakotas and east to the Allegheny Mountains. The dust buried the crops and suffocated the cattle and hogs. So much topsoil was carried away that the entire Atlantic seaboard was covered with a yellow, hazy smog. After a fact-finding tour of the Midwest, presidential adviser Lorena Hickok wrote:

> They've been having these dust storms, less intense, every two weeks

An Oklahoma family seeks shelter during a dust storm. The dust storms destroyed crops, forcing many farmers to abandon their farms and head west to California.

or so this fall. All this sort of thing makes for fear—and unrest. Some of the farmers I saw Monday looked frightened as children. Another thing that scares them is their debt load. They're afraid to borrow any more money. Their land, their homes, their machinery, their livestock—all mortgaged. They owe for seed loans, and, since they didn't even get seed out of this year's crop, many of them, if they go on, must borrow money for seed again this spring—if they can get it.[37]

Resettling the Desperately Poor

When conditions did not improve in 1934 and 1935, Midwest farmers had no choice but to abandon their farms and head west to California. There, they could not afford to purchase farmland of their own. Instead, they looked for jobs for a few cents a day as migrant farmworkers or became

tenant farmers and sharecroppers. Their living conditions were terrible, and there was a great deal of prejudice against these Okies from the Oklahoma dust bowl and tenant farmers who had been evicted from their Arkansas homes. Historian Robert Goldston writes:

Tenants and sharecroppers lived in a poverty which could only be measured against conditions in famine-stricken China or the poorest tribal villages of the Congo. Whole families worked in the field from sun-up to sun-down. They lived in broken-down shanties without sanitation, plumbing, heating, or windows. Their food was sowbelly [salt pork] and weeds; their diseases were pellagra, malaria, and malnutrition; their death rate was fantastically high.[38]

Eventually the Roosevelt administration, pressured by legislators from those states that were inundated with migrant workers, responded by creating the Resettlement Administration. The agency planned to relocate farmers, especially

Boys play outside a run-down New York City tenement. Millions of the nation's urban residents lived in dirty, crowded apartment buildings like this one.

tenant farmers, sharecroppers, and victims of the dust bowl, and give them a new start on good farming land. The government would supply them with equipment and seeds so that they could become independent, self-sufficient farmers. Although the agency hoped to move 500,000 poor rural families, only 4,500 were actually helped because the government did not have money to spare on experimental programs.

Life was not much better in the cities, where fourteen million people lived in crowded, unheated, unsanitary tenements. In a letter to Harry Hopkins, the director of the Civil Works Administration, Martha Gellhorn described the unemployed workers and their families:

This picture is so grim that whatever words I use will seem hysterical and exaggerated. And I find them all in the same shape—fear, fear driving them into a state of semi-collapse cracking nerves; and an overpowering terror of the future. . . . They can't pay rent and are evicted. They are watching their children grow thinner and thinner; fearing the cold for children who have neither coats nor shoes; wondering about coal.[39]

When they could no longer pay the rent and were evicted from their apartments, they used scraps of lumber and cardboard boxes to build shacks that they could live in. These new shantytowns on the edges of the cities were called Hoovervilles, for President Herbert Hoover, since many blamed him for causing the depression. In some areas government agencies could not be established quickly enough to take care of all of the needy, so many of them continued to depend on breadlines, where charitable organizations dispensed bread and soup or hospitals offered their leftovers. And relief payments were often inadequate. Lorena Hickok reported:

> There is no margin for clothing or medical service in the present relief grants to most families, and, while the present law continues, no cash for carfare, medical supplies, and the other small, but indispensable, household necessities. The inadequacy of the present food allowance under Home Relief is emphasized by the fact that prices have risen markedly, so that the same quantity of food that could have

been purchased last March for 96 cents now costs $1.10.[40]

Because of the accessibility of charitable and social service organizations, urban poverty was lessened. And the urban workers were far more likely than their rural counterparts to organize and to demand their rights. President Roosevelt supported their activities and advocated workers' rights. He publicly approved of the section of the National Recovery Act that recognized the right of workers to organize. The president said:

> When the businessmen of the country were demanding the right to organize themselves adequately to promote their legitimate interests; when the farmers were demanding legislation which would give them opportunities and incentives to organize themselves for a common advance, it was natural that the workers should seek and obtain a statutory declaration of their

A Hooverville in a section of Seattle, Washington. These shantytowns were named after President Hoover, who many blamed for causing the depression.

constitutional right to organize themselves for collective bargaining.[41]

Labor Fights Back

In its rush to standardize industry in 1933, the National Recovery Administration established a blanket code to be applied to all industries. It called for a 35- to 40-hour workweek in exchange for a twelve- to fifteen-dollar wage. The National Labor Board [predecessor of National Labor Relations Board], under the direction of Senator Robert Wagner of New York, was established to moderate labor-management disputes resulting from the codes, especially Section 7(a) of the National Industrial Recovery Act, which had raised the hopes of workers. It stated:

(1) that employees shall have the right to organize and bargain collectively through representatives of their own choosing, and shall be free from the interference, restraint, or coercion [pressure] of employers of labor, or their agents, in the designation of such representatives or in self-organization or in other concerted [coordinated] activities for the purpose of collective bargaining or other mutual aid and protection; (2) that no employee and no one seeking employment shall be required as a condition of employment to join any company union or to refrain from joining, organizing, or assisting a labor organization of his own choosing; and (3) that employers shall comply with the maximum hours of labor, minimum rates of pay, and other conditions of employment, approved or prescribed by the President.[42]

Business executives, however, continued to fight the efforts of workers to organize and negotiate for improved wages and working conditions. Some industrialists forced organizers out of town and threatened workers with violence if they joined unions. Although the union move-

---

Children and the NRA

Broadus Mitchell tells how the National Industrial Recovery Act affected children in Depression Decade: From New Era Through New Deal 1929–1941.

"The reduction in child labor laws was a distinct social gain. The President's Re-Employment Agreement forbade in most cases the employment of workers under sixteen years of age; this became the pattern in most of the codes. Reform of child labor has always been easiest in times of heavy unemployment; still N.R.A. is to be credited with a precedent which was influential until the extraordinary demand for workers during World War II relaxed standards."

Coal miners on the steps of their company store. Many industries controlled the lives of their employees by forcing them to live in high-rent company housing, and to shop in company stores where products were sold at inflated prices.

ment had gained some ground in the late nineteenth and early twentieth centuries, in its early years the depression had an adverse effect on union activities. Because of the scarcity of jobs, management could set its own terms and know that workers, who were glad to have jobs, any jobs, would agree to those terms.

Most Americans today cannot fathom the extent to which all industries controlled their workers' lives in the 1930s. Workers, especially those in the automotive, textile, steel, and mining industries, often had to live in company housing and were required to shop in company-owned stores. They could not get out of debt to their employers because the cost of rent and food was inflated to equal the amount of their wages. In the mid-1930s a writer for the Federal Writers' Project interviewed the wife of a northern factory worker to find out about their life:

He works every day from six in the morning till six at night in Mr. Hunter's brick plant across the tracks. Some days more'n that—twenty-four hours on a stretch. That's overtime, but it don't mean no extra pay. It's forty dollars a month straight, no matter what. . . . We have to pay four dollars out every month for this shack. Mr. Hunter makes the hands live close by the plant. And he gits ahold of that four dollars for rent before we ever see a cent of Hub's wages. This shack ain't worth four dollars a month, neither. Mr. Hunter won't do nothing toward fixing it up. If a window pane's broke, we do the putting in.[43]

Life was not much better in the mining towns of the South. The following is an excerpt of a letter written by a miner in Kentucky:

We are half fed because we can't feed ourselves and our family's with what we make. And we can't go to the cut rate Store and buy food most all the company forbids such trading. If you got the cash. But we got no cash. And the companies keeps their food stuffs at high prices at all time. So you can not clear enough to go anywhere. And if you do go somewhere [other than the company store] and buy food you are subjects to be canned [fired]. . . . I would leave Harlan County if I had only $6 to send my wife and boy to Briston, Va. and I could walk away— But I can't clear a dollar per month that why I am [still] here, that why hundreds are here.[44]

By 1934, however, the workers had begun to fight back, encouraged by the NRA codes. In that year alone there were eighteen hundred strikes in which workers refused to work and attempted to close down industries that would not negotiate with them. The increase in the number of strikes was followed by two new types of protest, the sit-in and the general strike. During a sit-in the workers remain in the factory but refuse to work. In a general strike all of the workers in a city go on strike in sympathy with those who are trying to reach an agreement with a particular company.

An Effective Strike

The San Francisco strike of 1934 is one of the most famous examples of a general strike. San Francisco's longshoremen, or dockworkers, were among the most exploited workers in the country. It was their job to unload the ships at the docks, but they were hired by the day, often for as little as thirty-five cents for a twelve-hour day, and they had no job security. They rejected the deal reached between the shipyard owners and their conservative union leaders, reorganized their International Longshoremen's Association (ILA), and went on strike. The owners were determined to break the strike and brought in strikebreakers—nonunion workers—to do their jobs. The longshoremen patrolled outside the dock area, threatening and beating the strikebreakers. Supported by the police and National Guard, the owners decided to use force. A bloody fight followed, and two workers were shot to death.

Twelve thousand longshoremen return to work following the San Francisco strike of 1934. The strike was extremely effective, resulting in an important victory for the labor unions.

Ten workers were killed during this bloody clash between police and Republic Steel mill workers. The fight broke out after the company refused to recognize the rights of workers to organize and negotiate.

That was when the ILA called for a general strike. The majority of the laborers in San Francisco went on strike against their employers. According to Robert McElvaine:

The strike was remarkably effective. A journalist described the city on the first morning of the shutdown: "No streetcars were operating, no buses, no taxis, no delivery wagons except milk and bread trucks which were operated with the permission of the general strike committee. No filling stations were open, no theaters, no shops." Many small storekeepers showed that elements of the middle class identified with the workers' goals. Signs appeared in the windows reading: "Closed Till the Boys Win." [45]

Roosevelt refused to alienate labor by intervening in the general strike, which ended on July 19 with the acceptance by both sides of a government arbitration plan. The final settlement favored the longshoremen's union and gave the ILA control over hiring.

President Roosevelt's refusal to send troops to break the general strike encouraged other labor organizations. Unions also began to see the value of having politicians on their side. They encouraged their workers to get involved in local politics so they could elect judges and sheriffs who were sympathetic to union goals.

The unions' biggest victory was the successful strike by the United Automobile Workers against General Motors in the winter of 1937. As a result of that strike, United States Steel recognized the Steel Workers' Organizing Committee. Workers hoped their right to organize would finally be recognized in every industry in America.

It was a short-lived hope. Ford Motor Company and the smaller steel companies continued to refuse to recognize the rights of workers to organize and negotiate. On Memorial Day 1937 ten workers were killed in a battle at a Republic Steel mill in Chicago. It was clear to workers and union organizers that the struggle would have to continue industry by industry.

Creating Jobs

Meanwhile, the government continued to create jobs for those who could not find jobs in industry. The National Youth Administration gave two million high school and college students, primarily from urban areas, part-time jobs to help them stay in school. Its goal was to keep teenagers out of the workforce so that they would not take jobs away from those who were supporting families. And it established a precedent for the section of the Fair Labor Standards Act of 1938 that prohibited child labor in interstate commerce. Until then many children as young as ten years old were sent to work, where they were exploited by factory owners, who paid them low wages and provided poor working conditions. Writer Robert Goldston reported that "children in Connecticut were earning 75 cents a week for fifty-five hours of hard work."[46] In southern textile mills it was not uncommon for fourteen-year-olds to earn five dollars a week for sixty-six hours of heavy labor.

A New Deal for the Arts

The Works Progress Administration (WPA), not to be confused with the Public Works Administration, replaced the Civil Works Administration in 1935. Its projects never rivaled the massive amount of construction completed by the PWA; however, it was responsible for constructing and improving 651,000 miles of highways, 8,000 parks, and 20,000 hospitals, schools, and public buildings. It also provided jobs for unemployed actors, artists, and writers through the project known as Federal

---

One Woman's Work

Members of the Federal Writers' Project interviewed Americans to compile an oral history of the time. In These Are Our Lives, *an anthology of these interviews, the wife of a mill worker and sharecropper describes her life.*

"I hoed seventeen acres of cotton by myself without one lick of help except for the little grass pickin' done by the geese, done my housework, and looked after three children. Many a night after supper I'd scour my floors or do my washin' and have it ready so's I could put it on the line before I went to the field at sun-up next mornin'. In gatherin' time [cotton harvest] I'd take my little baby to the field and put him in a wooden box at the end of a cotton row of a early mornin' when the frost lay thick as snow on the ground. Me and George picked every boll that went into eight bales of that cotton and I never got so much as two yards of ten-cent apron gingham."

One, which supported the arts through the Federal Art Project, the Federal Music Project, the Federal Writers' Project, and the Federal Theater Project.

The Federal Art Project hired artists and sculptors to create paintings and statues for exhibit throughout America. The one requirement was that the works should have broad appeal. Therefore, the content often reflected American life and legends. The murals painted on the sides of buildings and in federal buildings such as post offices and town halls are the best-known examples of WPA art. Many of America's most famous artists, such as Jackson Pollock and Willem de Kooning, began their careers by working for the WPA.

Meanwhile, the musicians of the Federal Music Project formed orchestras across America, performed for many who had never heard classical music before, and provided lessons for those who wanted to learn. The project's most lasting contribution, however, was its collection of American folk music.

The Federal Writers' Project was also given the task of preserving segments of Americana. The writers were employed to write a series of state guides, to do ethnic studies of Americans from various national backgrounds, and to collect and preserve American folklore and legends.

The Federal Theater Project's aim was to create a national theater and to use theater to develop an awareness of social problems through plays about the issues of the 1930s.

Taken altogether, the New Deal programs of the Agricultural Adjustment Act,

Artists with the Federal Art Project at work in a New York City gallery. The project's paintings and murals often depicted scenes of American life and legends.

the National Industrial Recovery Act, the Public Works Administration, the Works Progress Administration, and the Federal Emergency Relief Administration relieved some of the daily suffering of the rural and urban poor by providing them with enough food, warmth, and encouragement to help them to survive the Depression. But the economy itself stubbornly resisted all efforts to improve. Make-work programs had been created, but real jobs in productive and prosperous industries still eluded American workers.

5 The Debate Between Recovery and Reform

In spite of the billions of dollars spent on New Deal programs and on promoting economic recovery in America, over eleven million Americans were still unemployed in 1935. The American people were frustrated by the lack of progress. Roosevelt and the New Deal had raised the expectations of poor and middle-class Americans and had convinced them that the government would help them. Now many Americans were becoming interested in different economic and social philosophies. Roosevelt, too, was disappointed in the slow economic turnaround and wanted to try some new policies. According to Basil Rauch in *The History of the New Deal 1933–1938:*

> A fundamental change in the political philosophy and policies of the Roo-

A cartoon depicts FDR as a doctor delivering his bag of New Deal remedies to an ailing Uncle Sam.

sevelt Administration did occur during 1934. . . . These changes may be described in general terms of purpose and political philosophy. The primary aim of the First New Deal was recovery, while that of the Second was reform.[47]

The movement toward reform had been initiated by the debate in the country between conservatives who wanted to slow down reform and reduce government spending and liberals who wanted to speed up reform. But the reformers were spurred on by those who were not content with just promoting the economic recovery within our capitalist economic system but wanted to change the system completely. Three movements, in particular, tried to push the country toward radical economic reform: the Townsend Plan, the Share Our Wealth Society, and the EPIC plan. The large numbers of followers that they attracted and the depth of their emotional appeal surprised both Democratic and Republican politicians and led them to reevaluate their own positions.

The Townsend Plan proposed alleviating the suffering of older Americans by paying two hundred dollars a month to every American over the age of sixty who had no other income, had never been convicted of a crime, and had agreed to spend the entire amount within thirty days. Formulated by Southern California physician Francis Everett Townsend, the plan attracted a following of over three and a half million elderly who, as a group, had been particularly hard hit by the depression. America's change from an agricultural society to an urban one had caused an increasing number of problems for the aged. On the family farm there

Dr. Francis Townsend (left) outlines his old-age pension plan. Named the Townsend Plan, it proposed that Americans over the age of sixty with no other income be paid two hundred dollars a month.

had always been room for the elderly. However, as the census of 1920 indicated, the extended family that included the elderly had begun to split up as members moved to cities in search of jobs in industry. Suddenly many elderly had no place to go and no source of income. By 1935 eleven states had old-age pension legislation, but these laws depended on local, voluntary compliance and were basically worthless. Older Americans

> felt ignored by the initial programs of the New Deal. . . . The nation's elderly, especially those who had not worked in years, had watched their savings vanish in the banking panic and could no longer count on assistance from hard-pressed families and relatives.

Louisiana senator Huey Long founded the Share Our Wealth Society. The society advocated a redistribution of wealth in order to lessen the gap between the wealthiest and poorest Americans.

Social workers from coast to coast told mournful tales of aging men and women evicted from homes and apartments, forced to accept relief, and, when that ran out, reduced to scrounging in garbage cans for food.[48]

The anger of tenant farmers against the wealthy landowners who had taken advantage of the Agricultural Adjustment Act to evict them from the land gave birth to the Share Our Wealth Society, founded by Senator Huey Long of Louisiana. A well-known advocate for the southern poor, Long wanted to use income and inheritance taxes to limit the size of the fortunes that could be amassed by the wealthiest Americans. He proposed redistributing the wealth to provide five thou-

sand dollars for every family in America. When he formed a third political party, almost four million Americans, mostly small farmers and unemployed industrial workers, gave him their support.

EPIC—End Poverty in California—was created by the famous novelist and long-time member of the Socialist Party of America, Upton Sinclair. The Socialists were in favor of unemployment insurance, old-age pensions, and the nationalization of industry. EPIC wanted to take over closed factories and unused farmlands to allow unemployed workers to produce the clothing and food that they and their families needed.

The followers of Townsend, Long, and Sinclair, as well as the increasingly loud voices of Socialists and progressives who advocated political and social reform, put pressure on the Roosevelt administration. With the Republican Party maintaining its silence after its resounding defeat in the election of 1934, the Democrats became a moderating influence in the country. Through the New Deal, the Democrats had aimed to promote economic recovery but not economic revolution. Now, in order to survive, they would have to address those rising expectations within the current system.

The Elderly and the Unemployed

The primary thrust of the second phase of the New Deal was to provide for the elderly and the unemployed. Roosevelt decided to appease those who might be inclined to move from reform to revolution with the Social Security Act. It sig-

The American Demagogues

Senator Huey Long and Reverend Charles Coughlin, in addition to Dr. Francis Townsend and Upton Sinclair, tried to capitalize on the growing radical sentiments. In A Generation on Trial, *author Alistair Cooke commented on their source of influence.*

"America was still the land of the middle class, the largest middle class in the world. And it was left to them, to the wage-earners with their savings gone, the fore-closed farmers, not least the business men and small broken bankers, to all who had prospered in the twenties and still had energy to feel the outrage of betrayal; it was left to them to berate 'the system,' the bankers, and capitalism itself; it was they who spawned demagogues who proposed radical surgery on an America which, they said, had been poisoned by 'the bankers, the brokers, the politicians.' Huey Long in Louisiana, Father Coughlin in Michigan, Dr. Townsend and Upton Sinclair in California offered between them everything from a poor man's dictator and a capital levy [tax] to an old-age pension. For a short dreadful time these men were the real possible alternatives to a social-security act."

naled a major shift toward the acceptance of government responsibility for the establishment of permanent social programs.

That was a new concept for Americans, but it was not new in other parts of the world. Many countries had already implemented some type of social security program. Germany's Reichstag or parliament, passed social insurance laws in the 1880s. In America, however, social security had been firmly resisted for decades as being un-American. Americans still prided themselves on their self-reliance and individualism. When the Ohio legislature attempted to pass a social insurance act, it was denounced as the "most menacing and revolutionary" in Ohio's history, an "attempt to foist upon the United States foreign ideals and foreign practices" that threatened "complete disruption of our American system of individual responsibility."[49]

In June 1934, under pressure for more social legislation, Roosevelt appointed the Committee on Economic Security to develop a proposal for unemployment insurance, old-age pensions, and health insurance. After much debate the committee favored federal administration as the best way to make sure that workers throughout the United States were treated equally and that those who moved from state to state in search of work would not lose their benefits. The committee decided that the program should be financed by both the employers and the

A cartoon criticizes the Social Security Act for identifying people by their assigned number.

employees and that the money should be placed in a combined account controlled by the government, not kept in the treasuries of individual industries. On the negative side, this added payroll tax would take money out of the economy at a time when putting money into circulation was necessary for recovery. However, employee contributions were seen as a crucial part of the plan. After all, if workers had contributed to the fund, it was their money being held in trust for their future needs. The fund could not then be taken away by the actions of future administrations.

There was some concern that if the program was challenged and brought before the Supreme Court, the Court would

The Power of the Constitution

Historian Henry S. Commager in Documents of American History, *quotes Chief Justice Charles Hughes's opinion that the National Industrial Recovery Act was unconstitutional. Author John Major reprinted Chief Justice Hughes's opinion in* The New Deal.

"We are told that the provision of the statute authorizing the adoption of codes must be viewed in the light of the grave national crisis with which Congress was confronted. Undoubtedly, the conditions to which power is addressed are always to be considered when the exercise of power is challenged. Extraordinary conditions may call for extraordinary remedies. But the argument necessarily stops short of an attempt to justify action which lies outside the sphere of constitutional authority. Extraordinary conditions do not create or enlarge constitutional power. The Constitution established a national government with powers deemed adequate, as they have proved to be both in war and peace, but these powers of the national government are limited by the constitutional grants [rights]. Those who act under these grants are not at liberty to transcend the imposed limits because they believe that more or different power is necessary."

rule that a federally administered program violated states' rights and was unconstitutional. However, in defending the constitutionality of such a proposal, the committee wrote that it was

> fully aware of the limitations imposed upon the Federal Government by the Constitution. . . . The staff is convinced, however, that it should first seek out the most constructive proposals for old age security adapted to American conditions and then, only then, test as far as possible whether such proposals can be made effective within our legal system. Since law is a living science, it is reasonable to assume that if a sound program of old age security can be projected, our system of constitutional law will evolve in time to support that program.[50]

The plan that the Committee on Economic Security submitted to the president in January 1935 virtually ignored health coverage, suggested a combined state and federal unemployment insurance program, and proposed a national old-age pension funded by employers, employees, and government. Congress passed the bill, and the Social Security Act was signed into law in August 1935. Roosevelt admitted that it was not as far-reaching as he might have liked but pointed out that it marked a beginning:

> This law . . . represents a cornerstone in a structure which is being built but is by no means complete. It is a structure intended to lessen the force of future possible depressions. It will act as a protection to future Administrations against the necessity of going deeply into debt to furnish relief to the needy.[51]

Another major legislative initiative of the second New Deal was the Wagner Act, which signaled Roosevelt's final move toward a concession to workers. Because workers' rights to organize had been part of the National Industrial Recovery Act, the rights of workers in industries that did business solely within state boundaries were jeopardized by the Supreme Court ruling that declared the act unconstitutional. Officially called the National Labor Relations Act of 1935, the Wagner Act protected unions and workers who wished to form or join them. The law gave the National Labor Relations Board the power to prohibit unfair practices by businesses that did not wish to allow unions and to order and conduct voting to decide if a group of workers wanted to form a union.

Democrats' Popularity Regained

With the Social Security Act and the Wagner Act, the Democrats lured back to their party the workers who might have been attracted by Huey Long or Socialist and radical candidates in the 1936 election. In the 1936 presidential election Roosevelt again received his party's nomination. The Republicans nominated Governor Alfred M. Landon of Kansas, a progressive who had supported many of the New Deal programs when they were implemented in his state. Thus, he had no clear program to emphasize and found it difficult to criticize Roosevelt. FDR won the election by a landslide, winning every state except Maine and Vermont, and receiving 60.8 percent of the popular vote. The Democratic majority in Congress increased to

388 in the House of Representatives and 75 in the Senate.

New Dealers looked to the president to take advantage of those numbers and expand social legislation and economic reform. However, in August 1937 the recession of 1937–1938 began. The stock market fell; production, sales, and employment were down. By early 1938, 20 percent of American workers were again unemployed. A new depression seemed to occur.

A primary reason for the downward turn was a decrease in government spending. In 1937 the administration and Congress decided that recovery had been achieved. Production, stocks, and prices were up. It was time to balance the budget by decreasing government spending. The Works Progress Administration cut the number of people it employed by 50 percent, and the Public Works Administration almost ceased operation. In addition, the new social security program removed two billion dollars from workers' spendable income that year, as a result of the workers' starting to contribute to the system.

The president stopped sending innovative economic and social legislation to Congress and focused, instead, on preserving the reforms that he had already initiated and giving them time to work. He was worried that the Supreme Court would rule that many of the programs, such as the Social Security and the Wagner Acts, were unconstitutional because they limited the rights of states to set their own policies for working conditions, wages, relief programs, and pensions. In his effort to preserve the New Deal, Roosevelt sent one final, radical reform proposal to Congress: the Supreme Court Reform Bill of 1937.

Supporters cheer the renomination of President Roosevelt in 1936. Having earned overwhelming support for passage of the Social Security and Wagner Acts, FDR was easily elected to a second term in office.

Politics, Not Philosophy

Robert S. McElvaine explains the difference between the first and second New Deals in The Great Depression.

"Franklin Roosevelt was neither a philosopher nor an economist; he was a politician. Neither his programs of 1933 nor those of 1935 were based on a coherent ideological position [political philosophy]. Consistency troubled Roosevelt little. Votes were far more important."

The bill would have increased the number of Supreme Court judges by allowing the president to appoint a new judge for each one on the Supreme Court who had served for ten years and who did not retire within six months of turning seventy. On the surface the purpose of the bill was to make the Court more efficient and minimize the workload of the aging judges. But everyone knew that Roosevelt just wanted to appoint justices who favored New Deal policies.

Congress handed Roosevelt his first major defeat. In rejecting the bill, the Senate Committee on the Judiciary said that such a proposal would

> make this Government one of men rather than one of law, and its practical operation would be to make the Constitution what the executive or legislative branches of the government choose to say it is—an interpretation to be changed with a change of administration.[52]

With that decision, Congress, in the name of the American people, chose to seek economic recovery within the parameters of a democratic government and a capitalist economic system. The people's ultimate resolve to continue to base their government on the U.S. Constitution, not on momentary whims or crises, distinguished America from the other major powers in the 1930s. Looking back to that time, Franklin Delano Roosevelt, himself, commented:

> Most vital to our present and to our future is this experience of a democracy which survived crises at home; put away many evil things; built new structures on enduring lines; and, through it all, maintained the fact of its democracy.

> For action has been taken within the three-way framework of the Constitution of the United States. The coordinate branches of the government continue freely to function. The Bill of Rights remains inviolate. The freedom of elections is wholly maintained. Prophets of the downfall of American democracy have seen their dire predictions come to naught [nothing].[53]

6 The Worldwide Depression

In accepting the Democratic nomination for another presidential term, Roosevelt acknowledged that, unlike the United States, other countries had jeopardized their democratic ideals to solve their economic problems. He said:

> In this world of ours, in other lands, there are some people, who, in times past have lived and fought for freedom, and seem to have grown weary to carry on the fight. They have sold their heritage of freedom for the illusion of a living. They have yielded their democracy.[54]

The Great Depression of 1929 to 1939 was a worldwide phenomenon that resulted from economic and political decisions made immediately following World War I. With the exception of the Soviet Union, the depression profoundly affected each of the major powers: the United States, Great Britain, Germany, France, Italy, and Japan. However, after the failure of the World Economic Conference of

Ten thousand London demonstrators protest the British government's policies on unemployment in 1934. Most of the world's major powers were as hard hit by the depression as the United States.

International Hoovervilles

Hoovervilles were not only an American phenomenon. In The Great Depression, *John Garraty describes the international housing problem.*

"On the borders of cities from Adelaide and Sydney in Australia to Buenos Aires in Argentina, shantytowns sprang up as groups of homeless people constructed ramshackle shelters on vacant land. One of the most elaborate of these places was the Village of Misery on the northwest outskirts of Vienna, with its shacks made of broken bricks, rusting stovepipes, and other discarded building materials."

1933, there were no attempts to find solutions through international cooperation. Instead, nations followed the advice of British economist John Maynard Keynes:

> Ideas, knowledge, science, hospitality, travel—these are the things which should of their nature be international. But let goods be homespun whenever it is reasonable and conveniently possible, and above all, let finance be primarily national.[55]

Ultimately, this mutual distrust and isolationism resulted in World War II.

Throughout the 1930s the lack of cooperation was most evident in the area of agricultural production. Farmers in South America and Africa who had not previously been exporting wheat and grains were releasing a surplus of food products into the world market and driving prices down. To counter this effect, the farmers of the exporting nations tried to limit their own production. Beginning in 1933 restrictive policies were put into effect in many nations. In policies similar to the Agricultural Adjustment Act in the United

States, other countries also paid for the destruction of surplus crops or limited which crops could be produced. Meanwhile, the importing countries, mainly in Europe, tried to protect their own farmers through tariffs and subsidies, direct government payment to farmers for either producing or eliminating certain crops. There were some attempts at international agreement, such as the International Wheat Agreement of 1933 in which exporters agreed to limit their production of wheat at the level at which importers could purchase their crops. However, the overall effect was to damage the international balance of trade and lengthen the depression.

In addition, almost every nation, from Central America to Europe to Asia, had its own back-to-the-land movement in which residents of cities were urged to forget about regaining jobs in industry and move back to the country, where they could begin growing their own food. In Mexico, President Lázaro Cárdenas promoted a homesteading program in which landless peasants were settled on their own farms.

Banks were formed to help these new farmers obtain machinery, and village industries were encouraged. In Germany the life of the self-sufficient small farmer was praised, and tax laws favored family farms. In India land reform and the return to self-sufficiency was basic to Gandhi's political movement. Even the Roosevelt administration in America attempted some resettlement of the unemployed in rural areas.

However, these movements did not succeed. Industrial workers either had no interest in farming, or they lacked the skills to succeed in that area. Besides, in a world in which agricultural overproduction had lowered profits, established farmers were not making money, so unemployed industrial workers had an even slimmer chance of succeeding. As Canadian socialist J. S. Woodsworth noted: "In the old days we could send people from the cities to the country. If they went out today they would meet another army of unemployed coming back from the country to the city; that outlet is closed."[56] Resettling attempts failed to improve the living conditions of the people and only served to complicate the search for real solutions.

For the Third World, or underdeveloped, countries of Asia, this decline in agriculture resulted in industrial growth. When unindustrialized nations lost their income from agricultural commodities and the export of raw materials, they began producing those products that they had previously imported. As historian John Garraty has commented:

> The effect that unfavorable terms of trade during the depression had on unindustrialized nations was not always unfortunate. Quite the contrary, in many instances it caused beneficial structural changes in their economies. When they ran out of foreign exchange to pay for manufactures [manufactured goods], they shifted capital and labor from agricultural and mining to the production of cement, paper, soap, textiles, and other previously imported necessities. The process, called import substitution, was often carried out without plan by large numbers of small entrepreneurs. Nevertheless, it resulted in better-balanced economies and improved standards of living.[57]

This loss of Third World markets added to the industrial decline of Europe and America during the 1930s. In the 1920s industrial production had increased in every industrial country. Even though the rate of growth differed, the overall employment opportunities and wages of workers had improved. But during the depression millions of workers worldwide lost their jobs. Employed workers did not feel secure in their jobs and often agreed to work for lower wages in order to keep those jobs. As with the agricultural crisis, each country attempted to deal with its own problems in isolation. This resulted in worsening conditions.

Tariffs Tighten the Flow of Goods

Just as nations had attempted to protect their farmers through limiting food imports, they adopted tariffs to protect their manufacturers. The Hawley-Smoot tariff in America began as a tariff on agricultural products and was quickly expanded

Unemployed Germans line up at a Berlin soup kitchen during the depression. In response to ever-increasing poverty, countries like Germany and the United States stepped up spending for public works.

to include industrial commodities as well. Other nations followed suit, and soon each of the industrialized nations was limiting its imports through the use of tariffs and restrictions. As with the agricultural regulations, the main result was to cripple world trade. When countries stopped purchasing each other's products, they each lost markets for their agricultural and industrial commodities; sales fell, businesses closed, and even more people were unemployed. Free trade and an exchange of goods among nations would have provided more jobs for all workers, and every country would have benefited.

In spite of earning less money from taxes, at the beginning of the depression each nation tried to balance its budget and avoid deficit spending. No matter how different their political philosophies, world leaders, including Prime Minister Winston Churchill of England, Chancellor Heinrich Brüning of Germany, and Presi-

dent Franklin Roosevelt, extolled the virtues of the balanced budget. Even economists did not always agree that government spending was needed to get the economy moving again. However, when pressured by the overwhelming poverty of their people, each nation abandoned that balanced budget policy, and joined a third trend of depression economics: an increase in public works. In 1931 British economist Richard Kahn developed the theory of the economic multiplier. According to Kahn:

Employing the idle on public works would start a kind of chain reaction: those hired would spend their wages on goods, the producers of which would have to hire other unemployed workers, who would in turn spend their wages on other goods, and so on. The true cost of the public works would be quite small because the government would no longer have to support so many unemployed people and because the new workers would be paying taxes on their earnings.[58]

Spending for public works increased in the United States, Germany, Sweden, and Australia during the depression as a method of providing for the unemployed. But although it succeeded in decreasing the numbers of the unemployed and destitute, public spending did not have the hoped for result of producing thriving private industries.

Another trend was for unemployed workers to emigrate in search of a better lifestyle. At the very least, most countries, such as the United States, began to limit the numbers of foreigners who were allowed to move in. The Immigration Quota

Immigrants arrive in America in 1922. Many Americans feared that the increasing immigrant population would take up the few available jobs.

The World Economic Conference and Europe

In his Memoirs, *published in 1948, Secretary of State Cordell Hull reflected on the ultimate consequence of America's decision in June 1933 to concentrate on its own problems rather than on the international scene.*

"I believed then, and do still, that the collapse of the London Economic Conference had two tragic results. First, it greatly retarded the logical economic recovery of all nations. Secondly, it played into the hands of such dictator nations as Germany, Japan, and Italy. At that very time this trio was intently watching the course of action of the peace-seeking nations. At London, the bitterest recrimination occurred among the United States, Britain, and France. The dictator nations occupied front-row seats at a spectacular battle. From then on they could proceed hopefully: on the military side, to rearm in comparative safety; on the economic side, to build their self-sufficiency walls in preparation for war. The conference was the first, and really the last, opportunity to check [stop] these movements toward conflict."

Law of 1924 restricted immigration and set strict quotas to be in effect by 1927. Throughout the depression "America for the Americans" had become a popular slogan because people feared that immigrants would take the few available jobs. This international rejection of outsiders for economic reasons only served to move the problems of the unemployed from one nation to another and to make people more suspicious of each other. John Garraty states:

> The heartless refusal of many nations to admit Jewish refugees from Germany after Hitler came to power in 1933 was related to unemployment; the fear that the newcomers would either take jobs away from native workers or that they would become public charges overcame humanitarian sentiments.[59]

Socialism Grows

In spite of the similarities of raising protective tariffs, trying to balance budgets, funding public works, and limiting immigration, there were some major differences in the way the industrial nations experienced the depression and tried to solve their economic and social problems. Influenced by the riots and social unrest initiated by unemployed workers, the governments of Great Britain and France slowly adopted modified forms of socialism in which the government assumed ownership and control of essential industries and provided for the unemployed, the ill, and the elderly.

Great Britain survived the depression more easily than the other Western nations. It withdrew from the world economic

An unemployed protestor battles with British police in 1931. In response to growing social unrest, the government of Great Britain adopted a number of socialist policies.

scene and traded primarily with members of the British Commonwealth. Coal, shipbuilding, and the textile industry remained depressed in Great Britain, but production increased in mechanical, electrical, and chemical products. Agricultural tariffs protected British farmers and produced inexpensive food. As a result, the people were able to spend money on housing. The resulting increase in the purchase of household items boosted the British economy.

British citizens did not experience the crushing poverty common in the depression because an unemployment insurance and welfare system had been in place for almost ten years. British labor unions were a powerful political force that favored socialist programs that would take care of the working class during difficult economic times. All in all, Britain had no reason to seek international cooperation. According to economic historian Charles P. Kindle-

A portrait of Popular Front leader Leon Blum is paraded through the streets of Paris. The Popular Front achieved success in the French national election of 1936 with the promise of social welfare programs.

berger, "The British economy was comfortable during the 1930's, as it had not been in the 1920's, and the authorities were in no hurry to give up their freedom of action through international agreement."[60]

It was more difficult for France to face the economic problems of the depression because it also experienced political unrest. French workers wanted the social welfare programs that British workers had. Elections were repeatedly held as successive governments were removed from office because of their inability to solve the problems. In the French national election of 1936, the Socialists joined with the Communists to form a Popular Front, or coalition government. Led by Socialist Leon Blum, they won a major victory. Nationwide sit-downs, or strikes, throughout French industry shocked businesspeople into accepting the front's policies. The Popular Front was more moderate than its Socialist and Communist roots. Historian Garraty writes:

> The Popular Front program had many elements that resembled important New Deal policies. These included guarantees to labor such as old-age and unemployment insurance, enforcement of the right of workers to organize and bargain collectively, and a 40-hour work week. Blum also promised a public works program to stimulate the economy and create jobs.[61]

Industries throughout the world had bowed to pressure from their own workers to establish the forty-hour workweek as a means of increasing the number of employed workers. But in France, where unemployment was not the most pressing problem, the shortened workweek simply

Unemployment was virtually eliminated in Italy under dictator Benito Mussolini. The country's recovery was mostly due to a military buildup.

lowered industrial production and made it more difficult for France to compete in other markets. And France's economy slowly worsened.

Germany, Italy, and Japan attempted to solve their problems by changing their governments because these regimes guaranteed full employment. Unfortunately, these fascist regimes curtailed civil rights and dissent. They also employed workers by drastically increasing their militaries.

War Preparations Ease Economic Troubles

In Italy, Benito Mussolini had been given absolute power by 1933, when he announced a plan for a state-controlled industrial system known as the corporate state, or corporatism. Confederations of industrial employers reached agreements with their workers' organizations under the complete supervision of and regulation by the government. At a time when most governments did not seem to know what to do about the economic crisis, many Western businesspeople praised Mussolini's success in achieving full employment and regulating surpluses. Even Gerard Swope, president of the General Electric Company in America, advocated corporatism. In a speech to the National Electrical Manufacturers Association, he said, "Production and consumption should be coordinated . . . preferably by the joint participation and joint administration of management and employees."[62] He went on to suggest that American industry should be regulated by the Federal Trade Commission so that the United States, too, could enjoy a balance between production and sales and a decrease in the unemployment rate.

But a military buildup, not corporatism, was responsible for Italy's recovery. Many of those state-owned factories had been busily producing artillery, machine guns, poison gas, and military uniforms. And unemployment had been decreased by enlarging the Italian army.

German people gather around a cart where free food is being dispensed to the hungry. When Adolf Hitler came to power in 1933, Germany was in the midst of a devastating depression.

Then Mussolini needed a target for his military buildup. He chose to invade Ethiopia on October 3, 1935. Nine months later, when General Francisco Franco of Spain attacked the established Spanish Republican government, Italy joined him and provided him with weapons. With those actions, Italy had moved from economic peacetime recovery to a wartime economy and ended its depression.

In Japan, too, economic recovery in the 1930s was related to military spending. Japan was a prime example of an unindustrialized nation that had developed its manufacturing capabilities when demand for its agricultural products, especially silk, decreased. Like Italy, Japan had chosen a highly controlled domestic economy in which production and demand were carefully monitored. And, like Italy, Japan's economic success depended on its military buildup. Beginning with Japan's 1937 war with China, full employment was achieved, and the Japanese depression ended.

Germany, too, turned inward to solve its depression-era problems. On January 30, 1933, Adolf Hitler, leader of the Nazi Party, became chancellor of Germany. In his first radio address Hitler emphasized Germany's economic problems:

> The misery of our people is horrible. To the hungry, unemployed millions of industrial workers is added the impoverishment of the whole middle class and the artisans. If this decay also finally finishes off the German farmers, we will face a catastrophe of incalculable size.[63]

Hitler began trying to bring Germany out of the depression by regulating the economy. He immediately put into effect a four-year plan for rebuilding Germany's economy. This plan controlled food prices and production, increased the number of young men drafted into the military in order to decrease unemployment, increased spending on public works, including the building of the autobahns, Germany's highway system, and regulated wages and working conditions. The German government required all workers to carry a book like a passport, through which their employment and travel throughout the countryside was monitored. Support for the loss of individual freedoms was gained by giving workers benefits such as subsidized housing and recreational facilities. The result of such a highly controlled economy was a major decrease in unemployment, from six million in October 1933 to one and a half million German workers in February 1937.

However, the second four-year plan, introduced by Hitler in October 1936, changed the German government's focus from domestic recovery to preparation for war. Germany had joined Italy in helping Franco in the Spanish Civil War and was plotting to regain the territories lost by the German people as a result of World War I. By that time Hitler had consolidated his political power and was the sole ruler of Germany. Unlike the Socialists and Communists in Britain, France, and Italy, he had not yet nationalized important industries, but all industry was closely regulated. As historian Garraty has noted:

> After 1935 the increasing emphasis of the Nazis on preparing for war had much to do with the new restrictions on private business interests. They placed strict controls on imports in order to conserve the foreign exchange needed to buy raw materials used in the manufacture of munitions and other military necessities. These controls put nearly all industries at the mercy of the regime, whether they were making military or civilian goods.[64]

Hitler breaks ground for Germany's new highway system, the autobahns. The building of the autobahns was included in Hitler's four-year plan for rebuilding Germany's economy.

The German government also encouraged the further development of the rubber, oil, and steel industries in order to make Germany immune from embargoes and blockades. The government increased the number of soldiers in its army and encouraged investment in factories that produced military weapons and armaments. The resulting new jobs then put more money back into the German economy and brought Germany out of its depression period.

U.S. Recovery Linked to War

In the United States, too, preparations for war were the ultimate weapon against the depression. In light of the Spanish Civil War, Italy's invasion of Ethiopia, the war in Asia, and Hitler's threats against eastern Europe, even the normally isolationist United States felt the need to spend more money on defense. This increased defense spending accomplished what social welfare programs and public works had not: a decrease in unemployment and the establishment of new industries.

The beginnings and ends of economic eras are not usually marked with precise dates because economic trends are too nebulous, or indistinct. However, the Great Depression is an exception. The collapse of the American stock market in October 1929 marks its beginning. And Germany's invasion of Czechoslovakia in March 1939 marks its end. It was that act of aggression that caused the rest of Europe and the United States to begin the arms buildup and war preparations that would finally end the Great Depression in those nations.

Early in the depression, British economist John Maynard Keynes had prescribed

Germany's invasion of Czechoslovakia in March 1939 (pictured) marks the end of the Great Depression. The invasion prompted the United States and European countries to begin a military buildup that eventually led to an upturn in their economies.

government spending as the way to work a country out of a depression. The nations of the world had tried that in a limited way but had been too worried about government debt to completely give themselves over to such an experiment. However, they were willing to risk a deficit when they were threatened by military attack. In France government expenditures for defense grew from 50 billion francs in 1935 to 150 billion in 1939. Great Britain spent 1.4 billion pounds in 1939, up from 1 billion in 1938.

U.S. national security expenditures grew more slowly. However, in 1939 it spent $8.9 billion, more than twice what it had spent in 1934. And full employment was soon achieved in almost every nation.

As Leon Blum, the premier of France, had predicted in 1937, the surest way to end the depression was to rearm: "Around the manufacture of armaments, there will be coordinated an economy which will be the basis for a more abundant production in all domains."[65]

Chapter

7 The Legacy of the Depression

The United States survived the Great Depression with its democratic political system and capitalist economic system intact. But the fundamental outlook of the nation had changed. The New Deal programs created a shift in the relationship between the American people and their government. And the social and economic reforms instituted in the 1930s continue to affect our lives today. In his introduction to *The New Deal*, historian Carl N. Degler wrote, "Americans still live in the era of the New Deal, for its achievements are now the base mark below which no conservative government may go and from which all new reform now starts."[66]

The New Deal would not have been possible without the change in attitude that occurred during the 1930s. Before the depression Americans thought of themselves as self-reliant pioneers and businesspeople whose economic prosperity depended on the sweat of their brows. As Americans of the 1930s moved from a rural to an urban society, however, they were becoming increasingly dependent on each other. Historian Samuel Lubell noted the shift in outlook in his book, *The Future of American Politics:*

> To Herbert Hoover, the phrase "rugged individualism" evoked nostalgic mem-

ories of a rural self-sufficiency in which a thrifty, toiling farmer had to look to the market place for only the last fifth of his needs. . . . In the city, though, the issue has always been man against man. The wage earner had to look to the government to make sure that the milk bought for his baby was not watered or tubercular; he had to look to the government to regulate the construction of tenements so all sunlight was not blocked out. If only God could make a tree, only the government could make a park.[67]

But the shift away from rugged individualism was gradual. As late as 1931 the National Conference of Social Workers opposed the concept of relief payments to the unemployed. And it was not until 1932 that the American Federation of Labor first supported unemployment insurance.

However, the Hoover years of the depression, 1929 to 1933, clearly illustrated that when left to itself and the demands of the marketplace, business did not always produce the best society for all to live in. By the time Franklin Roosevelt was elected with his promise of a New Deal, the American people were ready to accept government regulation of business and the economy. They were willing to give up the

Thousands of senior citizens demonstrate outside the Washington Capitol in 1981 to save their social security benefits. Revolutionary concepts when they were introduced in the 1930s, social security and welfare are now viewed by many as basic American rights.

pride of rugged individualism for a safety net of social programs for those who were unable to provide for themselves. In *The Age of Reform* Richard Hofstadter wrote:

> Even before F.D.R. took office a silent revolution had taken place in public opinion, the essential character of which can be seen when we recall how little opposition there was in the country, at the beginning, to the assumption of the New Dealers that henceforth, for the purposes of recovery, the federal government was to be responsible for the condition of the labor market as part of its concern with the industrial problem as a whole.[68]

An Increase in Expectations

Before the Great Depression the people expected nothing of their government other than the common defense of the nation from foreign enemies. After the Great Depression, Americans accepted the con-

cept of what historian Carl N. Degler called the "guarantor state." Many of the reforms that seemed so revolutionary in the 1930s, such as social security and the right of workers to organize, are now part of the foundation of American life. Degler agreed with Hofstadter and Lubell when he wrote:

> To the old goals set forth by the Jeffersonians and Progressives the New Deal appended [added] new ones. Its primary and general innovation was the guaranteeing of a minimum standard of welfare for the people of the nation. WPA and the whole series of relief agencies which were a part of it, wages and hours legislation, AAA [Agricultural Adjustment Act], bank deposit insurance, and social security, each illustrates this new conception of the federal government. But the guarantor state as it developed under the New Deal was more active and positive than this. It was a vigorous and dynamic force in the society, energizing and, if necessary, supplanting private

enterprise when the general welfare required it. . . . To achieve that minimum standard of well-being which the depression had taught the American people to expect of their government, nothing was out of bounds.[69]

The Great Depression left two major legacies to modern America: a government-subsidized social security and welfare program and continuing government involvement in and regulation of the economic life of the country.

The New Deal's government-subsidized social security and welfare program is still in operation. The old-age pension provided by the Social Security Act is now the major source of income for Americans over the age of sixty-five. And it has been expanded to provide for their widows and widowers as well as for the disabled. Direct payment of relief money to the unemployed is still practiced. These are often referred to today as entitlement programs, a term that shows the extent to which they are considered to be basic American rights. Politicians sometimes speak of reforming the social security or welfare system, but they never suggest abolishing it altogether.

Government involvement in the regulation of America's economy is also an accepted fact of life and takes many forms. For example, before the Great Depression the government did not study the economy. Now, government economists are

How Secure Are Social Security Programs?

More than sixty years ago Europe and America responded to the depression by establishing social security programs. In a Time *magazine article of November 22, 1993, entitled "Farewell to Welfare," Jay Branegan considered the future of such benefits.*

"In a country just beginning to debate universal health care, Americans have long wondered how their allies across the Atlantic have managed to enjoy government benefits far beyond U.S. dreams. Now Western Europeans are discovering a brutal truth: they cannot afford them either. Everywhere on the Continent, the public and private welfare system is under assault. Governments are seeking to cut back womb-to-tomb protection for workers and the jobless, for mothers and children, for pensioners, the sick and the disabled. Companies pressed by global competition are trimming benefits. The steadily expanding safety net that had been one of the Continent's proudest achievements is starting to shrink. . . .

But they are not about to cast off these 'rights' so easily. Attempts to cut back on benefits and job security have resulted in violent labor protests in Italy and massive demonstrations in Germany."

employed to determine unemployment rates and keep track of the gross national product and currency rates. All of this is done to monitor the nation's economic health and to be aware of problems so that action can be taken to combat them.

The Securities and Exchange Act, which was passed in 1934 to protect investors from dishonest financial practices by stockbrokers and banks, is still in effect today. It established the Securities and Exchange Commission to examine the financial statements of companies that issue stocks and bonds to insure that worthless securities cannot be sold. It continues to regulate the American stock market in such a way that most economists agree that a failure like that of October 1929 would be unlikely today. Buying on margin is limited by law, and manipulating the market, through such activities as insider trading, is illegal.

The Federal Deposit Insurance Corporation, established in 1934, still protects depositors by insuring their bank accounts. Today accounts are insured up to $100,000 so that people do not have to worry when they put their money in banks. All national banks are required to join the corporation, and most state and local banks join it voluntarily. When customers see the letters FDIC displayed in a bank, they know that their money is safe because the government will reimburse them if the bank goes out of business. As economist John Kenneth Galbraith has noted:

> Federal insurance of bank deposits, even to this day, has not been given full credit for the revolution that it has worked in the nation's banking structure. With this one piece of legislation the fear which operated so efficiently

Depositors stand in line to collect their savings from the Federal Deposit Insurance Corporation after their bank failed in 1986.

> to transmit weakness was dissolved. As a result, the grievous defect of the old system, by which failure begot failure, was cured. Rarely has so much been accomplished by a single law.[70]

The depression proved that our government and our Constitution are strong enough to meet the economic and social needs of the modern world. At the same time, it was a national experience, shared by all Americans, that changed their attitude toward that government. In *Out of Our Past*, historian Carl Degler commented:

> The searing ordeal of the Great Depression purged the American people of their belief in the limited powers of the federal government and convinced them of the necessity of the guarantor state. And as the Civil War constituted a watershed [turning point] in American thought, so the depression and its New Deal marked the crossing of a divide from which, it would seem, there could be no turning back.[71]

Notes

Introduction: We Were Poor

1. Quoted in Studs Terkel, *Hard Times: An Oral History of the Great Depression.* New York: Pantheon, 1970, p. 20.
2. Quoted in Terkel, *Hard Times*, p. 93.

Chapter 1: The Roots of the Depression

3. Quoted in John A. Garraty, *The Great Depression.* New York: Harcourt Brace Jovanovich, 1986, p. 29.
4. Robert S. McElvaine, *The Great Depression: America 1929–1941.* New York: New York Times Book Company, 1984, pp. 34–35.
5. Charles P. Kindleberger, *The World in Depression 1929–1939.* Berkeley: University of California Press, 1973, p. 292.

Chapter 2: Hoover and Roosevelt

6. Herbert Clark Hoover, *The Memoirs of Herbert Hoover: The Cabinet and the Presidency 1920–1933.* New York: Macmillan, 1952, p. 204.
7. T. H. Watkins, *The Great Depression.* Boston: Little, Brown, 1993, p. 80.
8. *Report on the Reconstruction Finance Corporation*, quoted in Harris Gaylord Warren, *Herbert Hoover and the Great Depression.* New York: W.W. Norton, 1967, p. 22.
9. *Senate Committee on Manufactures, Unemployment Relief Hearings*, quoted in Warren, *Herbert Hoover*, p. 201.
10. Herbert Clark Hoover, *The Memoirs of Herbert Hoover: The Great Depression 1929–1941.* New York: Macmillan, 1952, pp. 153–154.
11. Hoover, *The Memoirs of Herbert Hoover: The Great Depression*, pp. 154–155.
12. Quoted in Warren, *Herbert Hoover*, p. 249.
13. Quoted in Richard Norton Smith, *An Uncommon Man: The Triumph of Herbert Hoover.* New York: Simon and Schuster, 1984, p. 144.
14. McElvaine, *The Great Depression*, p. 69.
15. Franklin D. Roosevelt, *Nothing to Fear: The Selected Addresses of Franklin Delano Roosevelt 1932–1945.* New York: Houghton Mifflin, 1946, pp. 4 and 12.
16. Roosevelt, *Nothing to Fear*, p. 13.
17. Roosevelt, *Nothing to Fear*, p. 21.
18. Frank Kingdon, *As FDR Said: A Treasury of His Speeches, Conversations, and Writings.* New York: Duell, Sloan, and Pearce, 1950, p. 224.

Chapter 3: The First Hundred Days

19. Quoted in Kenneth S. Davis, *FDR: The New Deal Years 1933–1937.* New York: Random House, 1986, p. 71.
20. Rexford G. Tugwell, *FDR: Architect of an Era.* New York: Macmillan, 1967, pp. 104–105.
21. Quoted in Davis, *FDR*, p. 90.
22. Paul K. Conkin, *The New Deal.* New York: Thomas Y. Crowell, 1967, p. 49.
23. Tugwell, *FDR*, pp. 95–96.
24. Quoted in McElvaine, *The Great Depression*, p. 152.
25. Quoted in McElvaine, *The Great Depression*, p. 153.
26. McElvaine, *The Great Depression*, p. 157.
27. Quoted in McElvaine, *The Great Depression*, p. 160.
28. Quoted in Davis, *FDR*, p. 192.
29. Quoted in Davis, *FDR*, p. 194.

Chapter 4: A New Deal on the Farm and in the City

30. Quoted in Watkins, *The Great Depression*, p. 13.
31. Quoted in Irving Werstein, *A Nation Fights*

Back. New York: Julian Messner, 1962, p. 118.

32. Quoted in Richard Lowitt and Maurine Beasley, eds., *One Third of a Nation: Lorena Hickok Reports on the Great Depression.* Urbana: University of Illinois Press, 1981, p. xii.

33. Quoted in Terkel, *Hard Times*, p. 93.

34. Quoted in Federal Writers' Project, *These Are Our Lives.* Chapel Hill: University of North Carolina Press, 1939, p. 240.

35. Quoted in Federal Writers' Project, *These Are Our Lives*, pp. 65–66.

36. Quoted in Watkins, *The Great Depression*, p. 194.

37. Quoted in Lowitt and Beasley, *One Third of a Nation*, p. 94.

38. Robert Goldston, *The Great Depression: The United States in the Thirties.* New York: Bobbs-Merrill, 1968, p. 155.

39. Quoted in James T. Patterson, *America's Struggle Against Poverty 1900–1980.* Cambridge, MA: Harvard University Press, 1981, p. 37.

40. Quoted in Lowitt and Beasley, *One Third of a Nation*, p. 49.

41. Quoted in Davis, *FDR*, p. 68.

42. Quoted in John Major, ed., *The New Deal.* New York: Barnes and Noble, 1967, p. 123.

43. Quoted in Federal Writers' Project, *These Are Our Lives*, pp. 224–225.

44. I. Berenstein, quoted in Major, *The New Deal*, p. 123.

45. McElvaine, *The Great Depression*, p. 228.

46. Goldston, *The Great Depression*, p. 57.

Chapter 5: The Debate Between Recovery and Reform

47. Quoted in Major, *The New Deal*, pp. 92–93.

48. Michael E. Parrish, *Anxious Decades: America in Prosperity and Depression 1920–1941.* New York: W. W. Norton, 1992, p. 328.

49. McElvaine, *The Great Depression*, p. 270.

50. Quoted in Davis, *FDR*, p. 453.

51. Quoted in Davis, *FDR*, p. 543.

52. Quoted in Major, *The New Deal*, p. 121.

53. Quoted in Kingdon, *As FDR Said*, p. 234.

Chapter 6: The Worldwide Depression

54. Quoted in S. Rosenman, ed., *The Public Papers of Franklin Roosevelt.* New York: Random House, 1938. Reprinted in Major, *The New Deal*, p. 99.

55. Quoted in Kindleberger, *The World in Depression*, p. 261.

56. Quoted in Garraty, *The Great Depression*, p. 83.

57. Garraty, *The Great Depression, p. 75.*

58. Quoted in Garraty, *The Great Depression*, p. 121.

59. Garraty, *The Great Depression*, p. 122.

60. Charles P. Kindleberger, *A Financial History of Western Europe.* London: George Allen and Unwin, 1984, p. 389.

61. Garraty, *The Great Depression*, p. 224.

62. Quoted in Garraty, *The Great Depression*, p. 149.

63. Quoted in Garraty, *The Great Depression*, p. 185.

64. Garraty, *The Great Depression*, p. 194.

65. Quoted in Garraty, *The Great Depression*, p. 246.

Chapter 7: The Legacy of the Depression

66. Carl N. Degler, ed., *The New Deal.* Chicago: Quadrangle Books, 1970, p. 27.

67. Quoted in Major, *The New Deal*, p. 209.

68. Richard Hofstadter, *The Age of Reform.* New York: Vintage Books, 1955, p. 307.

69. Quoted in Major, *The New Deal*, p. 213.

70. John Kenneth Galbraith, *The Great Crash.* Boston: Houghton Mifflin, 1972, p. 196.

71. Quoted in Major, *The New Deal*, p. 215.

For Further Reading

Russell Freedman, *Franklin Delano Roosevelt*. New York: Clarion, 1990. An award-winning biography of President Franklin Delano Roosevelt.

B. Glassman, *The Crash of '29 and the New Deal*. Chicago: Silver-Burdett, 1986. An analysis of the stock market crash and the various acts that made up the New Deal.

William Loren Katz, *An Album of the Great Depression*. New York: Franklin Watts, 1970. A book that emphasizes the problems of daily life in the 1930s.

M. Meltzer, *Brother, Can You Spare A Dime?: The Great Depression 1929–1933*. New York: Knopf, 1969. An analysis of the causes and effects of the depression from the stock market crash through the inauguration of FDR.

Ronald Migneco and Timothy Levi Biel, *The Crash of 1929*. San Diego: Lucent Books, 1989. A history of the stock market crash.

Works Consulted

Paul K. Conkin, *The New Deal*. New York: Thomas Y. Crowell, 1967. An analysis of the New Deal legislation.

Kenneth S. Davis, *FDR: The New Deal Years 1933–1937*. New York: Random House, 1986. An informative biography that focuses on the early years of the New Deal.

Carl N. Degler, ed., *The New Deal*. Chicago: Quadrangle Books, 1970. A collection of essays about the New Deal written by a variety of historians and reporters.

Federal Writers' Project, *These Are Our Lives*. Chapel Hill: University of North Carolina Press, 1939. This is an anthology of interviews with workers and their families conducted by the WPA in North Carolina, Tennessee, and Georgia during the 1930s.

John Hope Franklin, *From Slavery to Freedom: A History of Negro Americans*. New York: Knopf, 1967. Contains an excellent chapter on the depression's effect on black Americans in the 1930s.

John Kenneth Galbraith, *The Great Crash*. Boston: Houghton Mifflin, 1972. An economic analysis of the Wall Street stock market crash of October 1929.

John A. Garraty, *The Great Depression*. New York: Harcourt Brace Jovanovich, 1986. A good source of information on economic conditions outside the United States during the Great Depression.

Robert Goldston, *The Great Depression: The United States in the Thirties*. New York: Bobbs-Merrill, 1968. An account of the social, political, and economic problems of the 1930s.

Judah L. Graubart and Alice V. Graubart, *Decade of Destiny*. New York: Contemporary Books, 1978. A discussion of how the depression affected all levels of society.

Richard Hofstadter, *The Age of Reform*. New York: Vintage Books, 1955. Puts the depression into the context of the reform movements that preceded it in America.

Herbert Clark Hoover, *The Memoirs of Herbert Hoover: The Cabinet and the Presidency 1920–1933*. New York: Macmillan, 1952. An autobiography that gives the reader insights into Hoover's decisions.

———, *The Memoirs of Herbert Hoover: The Great Depression 1929–1941*. New York: Macmillan, 1952. An autobiography that provides insights into Hoover's decisions in dealing with the economic crisis and his opinions about the New Deal.

Cordell Hull, *The Memoirs of Cordell Hull*. New York: Macmillan, 1948. Provides excellent information about the World Economic Conference of 1933 and its effects.

Charles P. Kindleberger, *A Financial History of Western Europe*. London: George Allen and Unwin, 1984. Includes a thorough analysis of the worldwide economic problems of the 1930s.

———, *The World in Depression 1929–1939*. Berkeley: University of California

Press, 1973. A detailed analysis of the depression in Europe.

Frank Kingdon, *As FDR Said: A Treasury of His Speeches, Conversations, and Writings.* New York: Duell, Sloan, and Pearce, 1950. A collection of Franklin Roosevelt's most famous speeches and some of his correspondence to colleagues.

John A. Lapp, *The First Chapter of the New Deal.* Chicago: John A. Prescott and Son, 1933. Includes copies of texts of New Deal legislation.

Richard Lowitt and Maurine Beasley, eds., *One Third of a Nation: Lorena Hickok Reports on the Great Depression.* Urbana: University of Illinois, 1981. A collection of the letters of presidential adviser Lorena Hickok, who traveled throughout the United States during the depression to report on conditions and evaluate the effectiveness of New Deal programs.

Robert S. McElvaine, *The Great Depression: America 1929–1941.* New York: New York Times Book Company, 1984. An in-depth analysis of the causes, conditions, and effects of the depression on American society.

John Major, ed., *The New Deal.* New York: Barnes and Noble, 1967. A collection of speeches, newspaper articles, and government documents of the 1930s that tell about the depression and New Deal in the words of participants in New Deal agencies and journalists who covered it firsthand.

Broadus Mitchell, *Depression Decade: From New Era Through New Deal 1929–1941.* New York: Rinehart, 1955. A history of the depression years.

Ted Morgan, *FDR: A Biography.* New York: Simon and Schuster, 1985. An in-depth analysis of the life of Franklin D. Roosevelt.

Michael E. Parrish, *Anxious Decades: America in Prosperity and Depression 1920–1941.* New York: W. W. Norton, 1992. An analysis of events in America from 1920 to 1941, which includes the cultural implications of the Great Depression as well as the history.

James T. Patterson, *America's Struggle Against Poverty 1900–1980.* Cambridge, MA: Harvard University Press, 1981. Contains a chapter on the New Deal's efforts to combat poverty in America.

Franklin D. Roosevelt, *My Friends: Twenty-eight History Making Speeches.* Buffalo, NY: Foster and Stewart Publishing Company, 1945. A collection of FDR's speeches.

———, *Nothing to Fear: The Selected Addresses of Franklin Delano Roosevelt 1932– 1945.* New York: Houghton Mifflin, 1946. A collection of FDR's speeches.

Richard Norton Smith, *An Uncommon Man: The Triumph of Herbert Hoover.* New York: Simon and Schuster, 1984. A biography of Herbert Hoover.

Studs Terkel, *Hard Times: An Oral History of the Great Depression.* New York: Pantheon, 1970. A collection of interviews with survivors of the Great Depression about daily life in the 1930s.

Rexford G. Tugwell, *FDR: Architect of an Era.* New York: Macmillan, 1967. Background information on the New Deal by a member of FDR's brain trust.

Harris Gaylord Warren, *Herbert Hoover and the Great Depression.* New York: W.W. Norton, 1967. A biography of Herbert

Hoover that focuses on the depression years.

T. H. Watkins, *The Great Depression*. Boston: Little, Brown, 1993. The companion volume to the 1994 PBS television series on the depression.

Irving Werstein, *A Nation Fights Back*. New York: Julian Messner, 1962. An account of the New Deal and its effects on American society.

———, *Shattered Decade: 1919–1929*. New York: Charles Scribner's Sons, 1970. A good source of background information on the causes of the depression.

Periodicals

Jay Branegan, "Farewell to Welfare," *Time*, November 22, 1993, p. 22.

Brian Dumane, "Illegal Child Labor Comes Back," *Fortune*, April 15, 1993, p. 86.

Newsweek, "The Bailout That Never Took Place," June 7, 1993, p. 40.

Index

Agricultural Adjustment Act, 35, 49-50, 62, 81
Agricultural Adjustment Administration, 35, 45, 59
American Association of Social Workers, 27
American Farm Bureau Federation, 34
American Federation of Labor, 40, 80
Asia
  after World War I, 15
  industrial growth in, 70
  war in, 76, 78
Australia, 71-72
Austria, 69

back-to-the-land movements, 69
banks
  buying on credit, 17
  deposit insurance, 81, 83
  government loans to, 26-27
  international loans, 16, 18
  money withdrawn, 21-22, 25
  Reconstruction Finance Corporation (RFC), 26-27, 33
  Roosevelt closes for audit, 31-33
  stock market and, 19
  unregulated, 22
Bill to Maintain the Credit of the United States, 34
Black, Hugo, 40
blacks, farming in the South, 49
Black Tuesday, 21
Blum, Leon, 74, 79
Boulder Dam (Hoover Dam), 43

breadlines, 13, 48, 53
"Brother Can You Spare a Dime?," 12, 13
Bruning, Heinrich, 71
business
  controlling workers' lives, 55
  developed buying on credit, 17
  government loans to, 26-27
  National Recovery Act and, 40-44
  opposition to workers' organizations, 54-55
  producing luxuries, 17

Cardenas, Lazaro, 69
charities, to assist needy, 25-27, 38, 53
child labor laws, 40, 42, 54, 58
China
  Japan invades, 76, 78
Churchill, Winston, 71
Civilian Conservation Corps (CCC), 34, 44
Civil Works Administration (CWA), 39, 42, 52, 58
Committee on Economic Security, 63, 65
Conference for Continued Industrial Progress, 24
conservation
  Civilian Conservation Corps (CCC), 34, 44
  Tennessee Valley Authority (TVA), 36-38
Coolidge, Calvin
  support for American business, 17, 20
corporatism, 75
Coughlin, Charles, 63

Czechoslovakia
  Germany invades, 78

Dawes, Charles G., 16
Dawes Plan, 16, 18, 20
de Kooning, Willem, 59
democracy, 67, 68
Democrats
  government reform and, 61, 62, 65-66
  Roosevelt and, 29-30
Depression, Great
  affected the world, 68-79
  beginning of, 21, 78
  Black Tuesday, 21
  causes for
    hoarding money, 21-22, 32
    loss of world markets, 70
    stock market speculation, 19-20
    trade tariffs, 27, 69, 71
    U.S. foreign policy, 18-19, 72
    World War I, 15-16, 68
  charities, to assist needy, 25-27, 38, 53
  deaths from starvation during, 28, 51
  end of, 78
  legacies of, 82
  personal stories of, 13, 25, 39, 44, 48-51, 55-58
  programs to alleviate
    balanced budgets, 66, 71
    limiting immigration, 72-73
    military buildup, 75-79
    private industry, 24
    public works, 39, 42, 43, 58-59, 66, 71-72, 76
    tariffs, 27, 69, 71, 74

schools affected, 14, 43
time period, 12
weather's effect on, 50-52
Douglas, Lewis, 34
dust storms, 50-52

economic multiplier theory,
    71-72
Economy Act, 34
elderly
    change in families, 61
    pensions for, 61-62, 82
Emergency Banking Act, 32,
    33, 34
Emergency Farm Mortgage
    Act, 35
Emergency Relief and
    Construction Act, 27
employers
    take advantage of workers,
        49-50, 54-57, 62
EPIC (End Poverty in
    California) plan, 61, 62
Ethiopia
    Italy invades, 76, 78
Europe
    after World War I, 15
    depression affects, 68-79
    tariffs on imports, 69, 74

Fair Labor Standards Act of
    1938, 58
farmers
    Agricultural Adjustment
        Act and, 35, 49-50, 62, 81
    Agricultural Adjustment
        Administration and, 35,
        45, 59
    American Farm Bureau
        Federation and, 34
    as migrant workers, 51
    corn crops and, 35
    cotton crops and, 35, 50
    dairy products and, 35
    dust bowl and, 50-52
    Emergency Farm Mortgage

Act and, 35
food-price drop hurts, 25-
    26
foreclosures and, 26, 49
mortgages for, 16-17, 35,
    51
paid for not planting, 35-
    36, 69
paid to destroy crops, 50,
    69
paid to destroy livestock,
    35, 50
resettlement programs
    and, 51-52, 69-70
sharecroppers, 49-52
tenant, 49-52, 62
tobacco crops and, 35, 50
wheat crops and, 35, 50
worldwide programs for,
    69-70
farming
    electricity for, 37
    struggled after World War
        I, 16, 22
    tariffs on imports, 69, 74
    technology affects, 50
    Tennessee Valley Authority
        (TVA) and, 36-38, 45
Federal Art Project, 59
Federal Deposit Insurance
    Corporation (FDIC), 83
Federal Emergency Relief
    Act, 38
Federal Emergency Relief
    Administration (FERA),
    38, 39, 42, 59
Federal Music Project, 59
Federal Reserve Act, 31
Federal Reserve Board, 20, 32
Federal Theater Project, 59
Federal Trade Commission,
    75
Federal Writers' Project, 13,
    49, 55, 59
First Hundred Days (special
    Congressional session),

33
Florida Causeway, 43
food
    breadlines, 13, 48, 53
    prices drop, 25-26
    riots, 24-25
    souplines, 48
    supply exceeds demand,
        16, 22
Ford Motor Company, 57
France
    after World War I, 15
    defense spending by, 79
    effect of depression on, 68
    socialism in, 73-74
    strikes in, 74
    survived the depression,
        74-75
Franco, Francisco, 76, 77

Gandhi, Mohandas, 70
Gellhorn, Martha, 52
General Electric Company,
    75
General Motors, 57
Germany
    balanced budget and, 71
    effect of depression on, 68
    farming in, 70
    government benefits in, 82
    Hitler rebuilds economy,
        76-77
    invades Czechoslovakia, 78
    military buildup in, 77
    political unrest in, 20
    reparations for World War
        I, 16
    social insurance laws, 63
    spending for public works,
        71-72
Gold, Blackie, 44
Grand Coulee Dam, 43
Great Britain
    after World War I, 15
    balanced budget and, 71
    defense spending of, 79

effect of depression on, 68
socialism in, 73-74
survived the depression, 73-74
welfare system in, 74
world economic system and, 19

Harburg, E.Y., 13
Harding, Warren G., 17
Hawley-Smoot Tariff Act, 27, 70-71
health insurance, 63, 65
Hickok, Lorena, 42, 48, 50-51, 53
Hitler, Adolf
four-year economic plans of, 76-77, 78
hoboes, 14
homeless
elderly, 62
farmers, 51-52
Hoovervilles, 13, 52-53, 69
housing for, 30
middle class, 25
urban, 52-53
worldwide, 69
Hoover, Herbert
banking and, 20-21
loses election, 29, 30
nonintervention policies of, 25-29, 80
on government interference, 23-24
on Reconstruction Finance Corporation (RFC), 27
on starving people, 28
response to 1929 crash, 24
rugged individualism and, 80
World Economic Conference and, 45
Hoovervilles, 13, 52-53, 69
Hopkins, Harry, 38-39, 42, 52
Hughes, Charles, 64
Hull, Cordell

Memoirs, 72
hunger marches, 28
Hurley, Patrick J., 29

Ickes, Harold, 43
Immigration Quota Law, 72-73
India
land reform in, 70
industry
decline in, 70
growth in, 70
reforms for, 40-42
tariffs for, 27, 69, 70-71
transition from wartime economy, 15-17
International Longshoremen's Association (ILA), 56-57
International Wheat Agreement, 69
Italy
effect of depression on, 68
fascism in, 75-76
government benefits in, 82
invades Ethiopia, 76, 78
military buildup in, 75-76

Japan
effect of depression on, 68
invades China, 76, 78
military buildup in, 76
Johnson, Hugh S., 42

Kahn, Richard, 71
Keynes, John Maynard, 45, 69, 78-79

Landon, Alfred M., 65
Lange, Dorothea, 13
League of Nations, 18
Lindley, Ernest K., 45
London Economic Conference. See World Economic Conference
Long, Huey, 62, 63, 65

Mexico, 69-70
middle class
German, 76
hit by depression, 25, 63
New Deal expectations of, 60
problems in depression, 47-48
support for strikers, 57
minimum wage, 40-42
Muscle Shoals
hydroelectric project, 36
Mussolini, Benito, 75

National Conference of Social Workers, 80
National Industrial Recovery Act, 41, 42, 54, 59, 64, 65
nationalism, 18, 19, 69
National Labor Board, 54
National Labor Relations Act. See Wagner Act
National Labor Relations Board, 65
National Recovery Act, 41-45, 53
National Recovery Administration (NRA), 41-45, 54, 56
National Youth Administration, 58
New Deal
programs
Agricultural Adjustment Act, 35, 49-50, 62, 81
Agricultural Adjustment Administration, 35, 45, 59
Bill to Maintain the Credit of the United States, 34
Civil Works Administration (CWA), 39, 42, 52, 58
Civilian Conservation Corps (CCC), 34, 44

Economy Act, 34
effects on government, 80-83
Emergency Banking Act, 32-34
Emergency Farm Mortgage Act, 35
Federal Emergency Relief Act, 38
Federal Writers' Project, 13, 49, 55, 59
National Industrial Recovery Act, 42, 54, 59, 64, 65
National Recovery Administration (NRA), 41-45, 54, 56
Public Works Administration (PWA), 42, 43, 59
Tennessee Valley Authority (TVA), 36-38, 45
Works Progress Administration (WPA), 58, 59, 66, 81
second phase
focus of, 62-63
Social Security Act, 62-65, 66, 81, 82
Supreme Court Reform Bill of 1937, 66-67
Wagner Act, 65
New Dealers, 37, 66

Oettinger, Hank, 39
Okies, 51
old-age pensions, 61-62, 63, 65
O'Neal, Edward A., 34

Pollock, Jackson, 59
Ponselle, Elsa, 46
poverty
rural, 48-52
statistics on, 46

urban, 28, 52-54
President's Organization on Unemployment Relief, 27, 32-33
Public Works Administration (PWA), 42, 43, 59

recession, 66
Reconstruction Finance Corporation (RFC), 26-27, 33
Republicans
economic prosperity and, 23
government reform and, 61, 62
Hoover and, 29
Republic Steel, 57
Resettlement Administration, 51-52
Roosevelt, Franklin Delano (FDR)
as governor of New York, 30
balanced budget and, 71
cutting government spending, 34
effect of polio on, 29
election in 1933, 29-30
election in 1936, 65
"fear" speech, 31
fireside chats, 32, 33, 79
First Hundred Days, 33, 34, 44
first inaugural address, 30-31
New Deal and, 30
Nothing to Fear, 32
on American democracy, 67
on government regulations, 79
on Social Security Act, 63, 65
on Tennessee Valley Authority (TVA), 36-37

on worldwide democracy, 68
presidential powers, expands, 32-33
San Francisco strike and, 57
World Economic Conference and, 45

Salvation Army, 25
San Francisco strike, 56
Securities and Exchange Act, 83
Securities and Exchange Commission, 83
Share Our Wealth Society, 61, 62
Sinclair, Upton, 62, 63
Social Security Act, 62-65, 66, 81, 82
Socialists, 50, 62, 65
souplines, 48
South America
after World War I, 15
farmers in, 69
Southern Tenant Farmers Union, 50
Soviet Union
after World War I, 15
depression's effect on, 68
power struggle in, 20
Spanish Civil War, 76, 77, 78
Steel Workers' Organizing Committee, 57
stock market
crash, 21, 24
1937-1938 recession, 66
regulation of, 83
speculation in, 19-20
U.S. influence on world, 19
strikes, 50, 56-57
Sweden, 71-72
Swope, Gerard, 75

taxes, 35, 64
technology, 22, 50

Temporary Emergency Relief
    Administration, 30
Tennessee Valley Authority
    (TVA), 36-38, 45
Terry, Peggy, 48
Thirty Hour Bill, 40
Thomas, Norman, 50
Townsend, Francis Everett,
    61, 62, 63
Townsend Plan, 61
trade
    tariffs contributed to
        depression, 27, 69, 71
    worldwide, 15-18, 71, 74
Treaty of Versailles, 16
Triborough Bridge (N.Y.C.),
    43
Tugwell, Rexford G., 35, 38

unemployment
    benefits, 38-39, 82
    insurance, 62, 63, 65, 80,
        82
    in the cities, 52-54
    National Industrial
        Recovery Act, 42
    statistics on, 13, 24, 28, 60,
        65
unions
    American Federation of
        Labor, 40, 80
    child labor laws and, 40,
        42, 54, 58
    effect of depression on, 54-
        55
    National Industrial
        Recovery Act, 41-42, 54,
        59, 64-65
    National Labor Board on,
        54
    right to organize, 42
    Southern Tenant Farmers

Union, 50
    strikes by, 50, 56-57
    Thirty Hour Bill, 40
    Wagner Act protects, 65
    workweek and, 40
    see also named unions
United Automobile Workers,
    57
United States
    agriculture's transition
        after World War I, 16-17
    as creditor nation, 18
    business prospered in
        1920s, 17-18
    changes in society, 80-83
    as creditor nation, 18
    defense spending of, 79
    democracy in, 67, 68, 80
    economic crises in, 12
    economic exchange rates,
        45
    government
        balancing the budget,
            66, 71
        creates jobs, 39, 42-44,
            58-59
        decreases spending, 66
        federal deficit, 34, 45
        First Hundred Days, 33
        gold standard, 32-32
        prints more money, 31-
            32
        reform plans, 61
        regulation of business
            by, 40-44, 75, 80-83
            lack of, 20, 23-24
        social assistance
            programs, 25
        supports the arts, 58-59
    immigration to, 72-73
    income levels in, 39, 40, 42,
        46-47, 49

    industry transition after
        World War I, 17
    international loans by, 16,
        18
    isolationism of, 18, 20, 69,
        72-73
    military buildup in, 78
    production of luxuries, 17
    public works spending, 39,
        42, 43, 58-59, 66, 71-72
    stock market, 19-20, 21, 24,
        66, 83
    Supreme Court
        on National Industrial
            Recovery Act, 64, 65
        Roosevelt's reform bill
            on, 66-67
        *Schechter Poultry v. United
            States*, 43-44
United States Steel, 57

Wagner Act, 65
Wagner, Robert, 54
Wall Street crash, 22, 78
Wallace, Henry A., 50
West, Walter, 27
Woodin, William H., 31
Woodsworth, J.S., 70
workers
    right to organize, 53-54
    unions for, 40-42, 50, 54-55
Works Progress
    Administration (WPA), 58,
    59, 66, 81
workweek, 40, 42, 54, 74
World Economic
    Conference, 45, 68-69, 72
World War I, 15-16
World War II
    causes of, 69, 72
    demand for workers, 34, 54

Picture Credits

About the Author

Jacqueline Farrell received her B.A. in English and history from Annhurst College, her M.A.L.S. in American Studies from Wesleyan University, and a Sixth-Year Certificate in Curriculum Development from the University of Connecticut. She is a middle school teacher who lives and works in Connecticut. Her interests include writing, cooking, studying history, reading mysteries, and beachcombing.